White Crane Institute promotes the study of the role of gay sexualities and gender variation and orientation in the evolution, psychology, sociology, and practice of spirituality, ritual, and religion.

The Institute publishes **White Crane:** *The Journal of Gay Spirit, Wisdom & Culture.*

White Crane Institute's goal is to foster the gathering and dissemination of information about the critical role sexuality and gender have played and continues to play in the development of cultural, spiritual and religious traditions and to provide a nurturing environment for the continuation and expansion of those explorations for the greater good of all society.

Background

White Crane Institute is dedicated to researching, exploring and documenting the variety of spiritual roles and stories among contemporary GLBT and gender variant men and women.

By 'spiritual' we mean those actions and activities that provide a deeper and balanced connection to self, others and the world. This may entail work with or through established religions or it may be highly idiosyncratic individual study and pursuit. We will examine and study the dynamic of this tribe of people in the larger community and in various cultural contexts.

We seek to reflect, present and preserve the wisdom stories of the peripherals, individuals who have traditionally and universally served humanity as "bridge people," "mediaries," "culture carriers," "teachers," "clowns," "contraries" and "healers" or labeled as "queer" or "perverted" and to support their organic role in society.

Evolutionary theory affirms that nothing endures in Nature that doesn't provide some kind of adaptive behavior for the good of Nature as a whole. There is ample historical, scientific and anthropological evidence to demonstrate that GLBT people have been and are, critical balancing components in the development of healthy, integrated societies concerned with deeper values and spiritual community.

To demonstrate the innate, unique and spirited gifts that the often marginalized GLBT community plays in the development and life of humankind, White Crane Institute seeks to reclaim, through self reflection, scholarly study, and research, the traditional and natural stabilizing role of GLBT people in the holistic, spiritual evolution of contemporary societies and cultures in all its variety. We seek to educate, inspire, empower and unite through integration, not assimilation.

On the White Crane Spirituality Editions with Lethe Press

The most valuable asset taken from an oppressed people is their history. As a result, the GLBT community is a people constantly coming out of erasure. Because of oppression and bigotry, each generation seems destined to go through the same process of self-discovery, coming out, and finding one's place in the larger community.

White Crane is pleased to enter into a partnership with Lethe Press to make these classics of gay spirituality and culture available again to a new generation of readers. It is our hope that by making our rich history more widely and easily available, new generations can move beyond erasure, bigotry and hate and find their rightful role in the larger community of the world.

Bo Young
White Crane Institute

Dan Vera
White Crane Institute

Two Flutes Playing

a Spiritual Journeybook
for Gay Men

Andrew Ramer

with forward by Mark Thompson

ISBN 1-59021-023-9

Lethe Press
102 Heritage Ave
Maple Shade, NJ 08052
www.lethepress.com

Interior design by Bert Herrman and Sou MacMillan
Cover design by Sou MacMillan
Cover art, *untitled* © 1998 Paul Jermann www.pauljermann.com

Manufactured in the United States of America

102 Heritage Avenue, Maple Shade, NJ 08052
lethepress@aol.com / www.lethepress.com

www.whitecranejournal.com

Introduction

This book began in 1980, as a series of small channeled pieces. That's still a word I'm uncomfortable with, channeling. It implies to me something odd, weird, queer perhaps, so I ought to be more comfortable embracing it. A more accurate way to describe this book might be to say that it's a series of essays on gay spiritual life that came to me by listening to the still small voices that speak inside me. It's a received book, an inspired book, and I'm pleased to see it coming back into print in this series.

I've always been surprised by the letters I've received from men who were touched by this work, and by the ways that men have used it on their own journeys. For me this has always been a handbook for gay men in general, and two men in committed partnerships, specifically. But over the years I've gotten letters from around the corner and as far away as Wales and New Zealand, telling me that it's been used both with partners and in group sex rituals. Once I was leaving a new friend's house and turned to say goodbye at the top of the stairs, only to see my name beautifully inscribed above words from this book. He and his partner had used them in their commitment ceremony as their *Ketubah*, their Jewish marriage contract, without realizing that they had invited their author to dinner for the first time. Another time, I met a man at the annual Gay Spirit Visions Conference in North Carolina, who'd tattooed one of the glyphs in this book on the back of his neck (I couldn't resist licking it). As he was leaving the tattoo parlor, two straight men came in, liked what he'd done, and picked out two other images from the book to be inked with.

Two Flutes Playing ambles and rambles and babbles off in strange directions. But if you are patient with it you will find that there's an underground current, a spring of meaning, that runs through it. It's a book of love poems, a book of affirmations, a celebration of the love of one man for another, of a tribe of men for all other men. It's a story of our people, and I hope you will find it useful in your travels with love and toward love.

— Andrew Ramer
San Francisco, October 2004

The Sign of the Gay Tribe and It's Four Clans

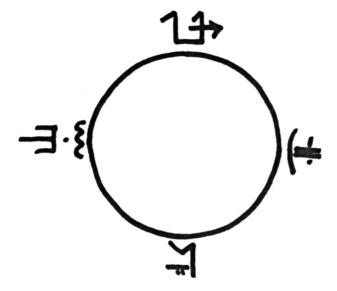

The scout clan is in the East, the place of air, of mind, of morning and spring.

The flute player clan is in the South, the place of water, the emotions, of noon and summer.

The shaman clan is in the West, the place of fire, the body, of sunset and autumn.

The hunter clan is in the North, the place of earth and spirit, of night and winter.

Table of Contents

Part Three: Priests of Father Earth and Mother Sky

Part Four: The Awakening of The Joy-Body

TWO FLUTES
PLAYING

Other Books by Andrew Ramer

little pictures
Tools for Peace
Angel Answers
Revelations for a New Millenium

with Donna Cunningham
The Spiritual Dimensions of Healing Addictions
Further Dimensions of Healing Addictions

with Alma Daniel and Timothy Wyllie
Ask Your Angels

Foreword

In a dizzying tumble of words about gay life that has left little uncovered, Andrew Ramer has something new to say. He does not rationalize, analyze, cheerlead or scold, but presents a simple vision so steeped in age-old wisdom that it appears more contemporary than tomorrow's headlines. By writing as purely from the heart as he does, Ramer engages a timeless place within us—a place beyond damage and doubt, caution and guile. Plunging fearlessly into the truth as he sees it, Ramer can't help but liberate readers from their own blinders about the saving grace of being queer.

He presents neither an argument for superiority or exclusion, merely a case for understanding the qualities he sees as inherent to those society has negatively labeled as "other." In fact, it is those very elements of otherness which give gay people their potency—if only they were to know it. Ramer speaks of queer folk fitting in, of finding their rightful place in today's world, but not from the assimilatory "peace at any price" posture espoused by many advocates of gay life. Pleading tolerance and social justice is one thing, striving to create a new mythic paradigm in which we can re-envision ourselves completely is another.

Ramer does not plead but rather patiently explains. He believes that the kinds of people now contained within the relatively short-lived but falsifying rubric of homosexuality have walked the earth from earliest times. Only they've had more honored names than today. Rather than live as outcasts or useless pariahs, these individuals had necessary tales to tell and vital roles to perform which advanced the human story. By trivializing the potential kept locked inside every queer life, modern society is wasting an invaluable part of itself. But Ramer's primary concern is less about saving a culture from its wrong-headedness than in restoring to those what was taken: a correct sense of place and purpose.

Some might say that Ramer's vision is naive, ingenuous at best. Where are the facts, the hard data to buttress his claims? The series of essays you hold here could be easily dismissed as no more than a fabulist's pillow book— a compendium of wishful dreaming. But it's because his writing has the insistent quality of a recurring dream that we should pay attention. If nothing else, Ramer has dropped a forward sounding into the depths of the gay collective unconscious.

He is not the first to do so, of course. Ramer is but one more voice in a long lineage of mystics, poets, and thinkers exploring the mysteries of those who sit at the edge of tribe; those whose status as outsiders makes them the ultimate insiders. We see—indeed, we're seers—beyond the norm, but not in ways which makes us any less a part of humanity's whole cloth. Our vantage, in fact, makes us an essential part of the weaving, adding durability, texture, and, without a doubt, color.

Whether Ramer's vision be interpreted as historical fact or speculative fiction should be less a concern than how it moves us now. He is a storyteller cut from a grand tradition. His words have the capacity to warm our hearts, stoke our souls, just as countless others have done before. However heard, there is no denying the heated urgency of Ramer's voice. In chill times such as these, we need the fire.

Mark Thompson
Los Angeles, January 1997

Introduction

When I came out in Berkeley in 1972, in the first wave of the gay rights movement after the Stonewall Uprising, I was looking for love and looking for a sense of who I was, where I came from, and why I existed as a man who loves men. In the political groups I belonged to, in the marches I went to, I found a sense of community, but did not find any answer to those questions. I did not find them in bars or discos. I did not find them in the first books on gay subjects that were starting to appear. I found a sense of power and purpose in those years, found love and heartbreak, but I never found anyone who could tell me the stories of myself and of my people.

At the time I didn't know I was asking spiritual questions, and did not know that others were also asking them also. In despair at finding external answers, I did what others were doing in that era of drugs and meditation— I turned inward. Since early childhood I had heard voices in my head, but by the time I was five I knew that grown-ups did not, and that anyone who did was considered crazy. I'd tried to make my voices go away, but I was no more successful at that than I had been at changing the direction of my sexual desires. But coming out had been empowering for me, and in 1976 I finally began to pay attention to my voices as well. For the first time, I discovered a source of information for all my questions. Like an ancient scribe, I began to write down what I heard, filling notebook after notebook with information about the roots of Western gay history and gay consciousness.

When I began this book I hadn't read Arthur Evans' *Witchcraft and the Gay Counterculture*, Mitch Walker's *Visionary Love*, Walter Williams' *The Spirit and the Flesh*, Mark Thompson's *Gay Spirit*, or Randy Conner's *Blossom of Bone*. Having read them I now recognize my journey and this book as solidly a part of our gay history. As men who walk between genders, we were seen in cultures all over the planet as also being able to walk between matter and spirit, the living and the dead, bringing back wisdom for all the people.

I call this a journeybook. It's not something to read from cover to cover at the beach. Part prose and part poem, its language is at times repetitive and convoluted, on subjects ranging from love to sex to gay mythology and tribal wisdom. The words of this book, like a shamanic chant, are designed to take you out of your normal waking sense of consciousness and into a different realm. There are exercises and meditations in each section, some that you can do alone, and others for you to do with a partner, for this is a book for gay lovers, to be read slowly, perhaps out loud.

You do not have to believe that the first part of the book, begun in 1980, just before AIDS entered our lives, comes from a man named Yamati who died more than ten thousand years ago. That the second section, written between 1985 and 1987, comes from Arrasu, who lived his last life during the Renaissance. That the third section, written between 1987 and 1991, was dictated by an angel named Sargolais. Or that the last section also came from Sargolais, between 1992 and 1995. Spirit guides, angels, or a deep part of myself, the source of this book doesn't really matter. This is a book of stories, to be read around the campfire of your own curiosity about who you are, why you are, and where we're all going. It's a complement to the journey of coming out. This is a book about Coming In, coming in to yourself, coming in to love, and coming in to who we are as a people, ancient, timeless, and renewing ourselves.

Andrew Ramer
Menlo Park, March 1997

Part One:
Two Flutes Playing

The Spirit of Man Love

Begin with the sound. Two flutes play. Water pours over itself, in the confluence of two streams. Candle burns beside candle. Their flames merge, lighting a darkened room. Two flutes play. Their notes circle in and around each other. This is the way of man-loving-man love. A special love. Deep and ancient.

In a world of two sexes, we know the magic of man and woman loving. We know of yin and yang, of heaven and earth, of night and day. We carry that, all of us, we carry that in our bodies. But what of man-to-man love? Of two together, face to face, bodies a sheath of the same vibration? What can we say of that love, which binds two men, which touches the union, the genderless heart of each? For all love is that, genderless. But what of the love where sheath is like sheath?

In the midst of two mirrors, eternal space replays itself forever. When man reaches out to man across the gulf of alienating space, eternity echoes in its forever. Two flutes play. And they dance. And the music changes. In the love of man for man, the unity of the cosmos affirms itself. And in a world of two sexes, were it not for that sacred bonding, your species would unhinge itself into warring halves. A mystery. That men and women can come together in their loving because men love men, because women love women. Same-sex love affirms unity. Without that affirmation, men and women could not meet. Their polarities would unhinge them, each from each.

In a world of two sexes, however different they are from each other, each sex bears within it the fullness of humanity. Where there is one human, female or male, in their heart, all of humanity lives. This is a paradox, that part is the same as the whole. But it is true. In a world of two sexes, where woman is, man is suggested. Where man is, woman is remembered. So that whosoever pulls away, man to man or woman to woman, from the mainstream of woman to man communing, in their closeness the fullness of humanity will flower, if they cast away fear, if they allow twoness to happen. For in their love, in their oneness, they are reminders to everyone of the fullness that every man and every woman carries. Sometimes it is easier to see the whole when part is not present, as men and women may forget when they dance their dance of bodies. Love between men can remind the world of that.

In a world of two sexes, where deities have been two-sexed, where language has two sexes; in the world, when two men meet they unlock the depths of their beings, mingle their hearts, each to each. In a world of two sexes, when two men meet in love they open a channel of communication to worlds, to realities where there is only one sex, to god-worlds, to planets of one-sex people. For too long humanity has explored the inner and outer two-sex realities. Love between two men is a leap, a door, a channel, for bringing new information about the greater reality into your world. Because there are one-sex realities, seeking a familiar vibration on your world through which to mingle love and understanding, through words, or through the passage of pure energy. In the love between two men, two flutes play, and this mingling happens. The song contains the mysteries, the joys of other places.

Love is genderless. Love is an energy that freely flows. In the end it does not matter who loves who. For the energy that fills the space between them is what matters.

Our culture divides the world into material and spiritual aspects. We see the material as being lower, base, sexual, the spiritual as higher, purified, sexless. Yet poets tell us there is one world only, whose aspects flow each into the other. Solomon's Song of Songs is both a sexual ode and a spiritual one, a song of lust and a song of the love of a people for its God. For the ancients, there were sacred marriages where mortals married god-priests or embodied goddesses. In Eastern tantric rites sex is used to awaken the divine energies in the body. So I would like to speak now of the spiritual tool that man loving man can be.

First there is silence. Then the echoing of eternity between two equally turned faces. Then there is the coming together of like bodies. Flesh partaking of the union. Eyes like fire. Lips like the sea. A forest of hair. The flight of birds. The swiftness of a gazelle in the heartbeat, in the touch of each to each. Oneness, oneness echoing. Echoing in the space between. And as the passion rises, as the energy rises, walls collapse and the spirit moves freely. Moves outward. Moves into vaster, still vaster places. And the boundaries of inner and outer are broken. Two lovers are alone. The world is gone. The sights, the sounds are gone. And in their hearts they know—they are the world, they are all. Whoever is the world, who knows that they are the world, touches the divine—in themselves, in everyone. And their bodies thrust and sigh and need. And then they burst, they explode. Swimming, lost in those moments of darkness. Of deep, of silent darkness. In the unleashing of that primal nothingness we all carry within us. The void, the great nothing from which the universe arose, wrapped in its mysterious holiness. We are sustained, we are nurtured in that returning to the source again. Swimming in nothingness. Weaving it into our present. And two men who cherish each other, who hold each other in those moments, they nurture in its memory, they nurture in its re-enacting, the primal birth of somethingness from nothing. Is this base? Is this vulgar? No! Divine this is. To cherish, to hold, to embrace the inheritance of time, of time born out of timelessness.

The male body vibrates differently than a female body. Their patterns of energy are different. So a male and a female body create a different pattern of combined energy in their meetings than the union of man and man, or of woman and woman. Once all religions knew this. The energy of those exploring the male-female path emerges in spirals. Woman to woman energy expands outward in rippling circles. The energy of man-to-man love creates a pillar, a column, a tree of living light, of liquid fire rising. So the spiral, the circle, the line. The differing faces of oneness. The bowl, the jug, the plate shaped out of clay. The ancients knew this. And this knowledge surfaces and resurfaces through time. Sometimes hidden, sometimes secret, still it lives on in the heart of humanity. Surfacing, going into hiding, waiting for the time when it can flow freely again. So twice in recent western history this knowledge began to surface, in Greece and during the Renaissance. But the world was still too fearful, too bound to childbreeding, to survival, to fully sanction the three patterns of love that it carries within. So as a bird carries the dream of flight, in our time a bird ready for flight spreads winged memory and sails into the blueness.

I speak now, and others like me speak in other places. We speak of the fullness of human life, the multiple paths, the differences. We speak of the common love-heart that births us all, living and loving in spirit. We come to a new time, a rich time. Let music play. Let music be played freely. Let new-fashioned ancient songs be played. The song of two flutes will now be heard again. The light-water-love song. The forgotten mystery. The teaching phallus. Not the knife, not the sword. But the candle, the finger that points, the walking stick. Two flutes play. There is no written music. No recorded song. Two men care. And in their caring, liquid flows the music. The energy is the same. How it manifests itself is different, as it moves between different places, between two who give out and take in. For a society to be whole it must encourage the flow of the three kinds of music. For together they make up the rhythm of your species. The three-fold, two-sex, one-souled people.

Two flutes play. Column of light. Column of water. Flowing neither up nor down. Flowing both ways simultaneously. Two flutes play. And their music creates light-column. Teaching column. Healing staff. Two flutes play. Rise. Making their deep shared music.

I speak of this music. Of the songs created by two loving men. Of the energy path that is created by their loving. Which links upper and lower, inner and outer. I speak of two men, but this music begins alone, with a man alone in his solitude, exploring himself, experiencing himself. Alone, and not hiding from his aloneness. Alone, and not afraid to be lonely. A man who pivots on the axis of himself. A man who is tender with the world. Who creates. Who is not afraid to wait. A man who feels within him the divine. Who feels the spark of life within him. And who reaches out to another man, not because he is afraid of the spark and wants to be distracted from its call. Who reaches out to another man, not with eyes, not to image, but who sees with heart-sight, from the inner eye. Who feels, not sees, the beauty in another man. Who responds to the outflow of energy in himself. Who can recognize that he has met another man whose energy is outflowing also. And two who have been alone, who have struggled and worked, they reach out and feel the energy flow both ways. For it must flow both ways. Yet it cannot be made to flow. It either happens or it doesn't happen. The solitary flute player, he will hear, he will feel the difference. He will know. Two flute players, from their solitude, will be able to hear the songs of each that echo, that answer, that spiral as they flow.

Love is light-bearing. The greater the channel, the fuller is the light-flow. The greater the channel, the more connections there are in your world. Between humans and animals and nature. With more connections comes more understanding. And with more understanding comes unity. You humans speak of yourselves as advanced. Yet the least among ants is more aware of global changes of light, season, air than you are. For with all your machines you have lost the sense of unity. In some respects you are the least among creatures. Who else needs speech as you do to communicate? Needs clothes and shelter for protection? You have yet to learn the union with the whole that an oak tree knows. The openness. The love.

Love is not heart-pounding lust, waiting by the telephone. Love is a soft feeling, light as air. It fills rooms, it flows from the heart. One flute player learns love, in his making music, in the making of himself into who he is. Then two flute players share, they make their common music. And in the song, the chant, in the spaces between notes, in the silence within and around them, two men can create the transmitter/receiver for union with the world. If the world is not there in their meeting, the flow, the ebb, the vastness, it may be need or lust or what is called love, but it is not love as I speak of it. Love is sense of union.

Sit quietly on the floor. Begin with that. The quiet. Legs crossed. Or sit in chairs. Sit face to face. Two who would make music. Two who seek to fill the world with the sounds of flute playing, who seek to fill the world by being full with it. Relax. Lightly touch knees and hands. Then begin a sound meditation. In which you let go of your bodies in making sound. There being no end but the sound itself. The humming, the chant, the droning. The risk in the making of whatever sounds the voice box makes. Two making this together. Two different rhythms. Now moving separately. Now playing off each other. Now following the same path. Deepening. Expanding. Until your bodies are filled with sound. Rising like smoke from an altar of sacrifice. Making sounds till they fade out by themselves. Each man learning to open himself, to trust the sound. To be free with his lover. Each man learning to share with sound the touch, the closeness, the separateness and mingling. To use sound as you have learned to use sex. Slowly learning to expand your awareness of self, or friend. Droning like a bee, hissing like a snake, full mouth open to cry out perfect wordlessness. The rustle of wind in trees, or the roaring of the sea. Be empty of self. And let the vastness of the world make sound upon you. This makes union.

Sit again, for this the second sound meditation. Sit, two, the same way. Face to face, relaxed. Opening your mouths wide, open your throats. Let sound pour forth in a single wide, thick, sky-ascending column. Make the sound of "Ahh." A loud "Ahh." Full body shaking "Ahh." Feel sound rise up between, surrounding you. In a vast sound column. And then, when the body-breath expends itself, listen to the silence that follows it. The falling water sound of silence after "Ahh." Its descent. Dropping. Moving through the body. Reaching a point of silent depth. Now, let sound rise up again. Up through the body. From pelvis to crown. Up above it. Sound of "Oh" this time. Rising. Rising. Two flutes sound. Two men. "Oh." Rising. To the highest point. Then falling into silence, into "Oh"'s descent. Now, begin again. This time with the sound of "Eee." Deep in the head. Chant rising. Rising. Then falling into silence. Slowly. With great spaces of silence between the chants. "Ahh. Oh. Eee." Rising and falling. Full bodied, full breath. This, a second sound meditation. Chanting these sounds over and over and over again. Till the electric walls of flesh are aquiver with connected sense of the man-man divine body oneness.

The sharing of sex, the giving and taking, they have for so long been looked down upon in the spiritual world. Celibacy has been praised, or the love of a man and a woman. Sex has been seen as evil, as falling, sin, distraction from the spiritual. And I say sex can be those things. But it can also be joyous, a delight, an opening of the senses, an opening of the deepest channels of light-bearing. Instead of orgasm being a downward flow of energy, draining the body and closing the senses, it is also possible for it to be an upward, outward flow. Drawing energy upward, nourishing the body center, filling the body, flooding the whole. Leaving the body like a fountain, from the top of the head.

The energy body is an interlocking system. A system of fire and water transmuted into pure light. A column of water runs up through the body from groin to crown. And two columns of fire run up through the legs, out through the hands, that burn in the nipples and surface in the eyes. The energy body is a system of fire and water. In the movements of sex, in the loving act. each column is open at both ends. So that fire and water flow, mix, mingle and are transformed. So that the body is transformed. Into a being of luminous liquid fire. Of liquid fire glowing. Light flowing wet. Fire going beyond itself. Water endlessly pouring. A union of elements. That in their opposition are transmuted. Love transmutes fire and water. Turns them into light. And when the light body is glowing, when the body is open in its circuits, then it is giving out more, receiving more. Moving toward union.

Crown of light. Two bodies of fire and water transformed. In the giving of liquid fire. The sharing of luminous delight.

Fire bearing channels. Water bearing channels. Light bearing. Ears open to sound. Eyes carrying fire. Hands spreading light. As lover touches lover. Each touch a caress. Each touch a key. Unlocking, opening the body. Slowly. In movements holy and embracing. Two flutes play. Two men open.

Light giving. Light receiving. The light of orgasm a liquid-fire gift. In the act of giving semen, a garment of light is given. A shield, a protection, "Cover me." a lover says. "I cover you," his lover answers, "in a garment of light, a garment of love energy."

In the giving and receiving of liquid-fire, the circuits of water are transformed, are opened. "I give you liquid-fire," says the lover. Passing light energy to his lover. And from below, the column rises. In him, in his lover. The energy of orgasm rises. In the one who opens. Energy rises upward. Opening and cleansing. Rising up through the body. Rising up and pouring out like a fountain through the top of his head. So that each is blessed in the giving. And when two open together, in circles, the energy cleanses. The waters above and the waters beneath, the waters of one and the liquid-fire waters of the other are united. The bodies—united. The circuits are open.

The giving of light into darkness. The giving of liquid-light into the source of light which is darkness. In the giving and receiving, meditate. Prepare yourselves. Feel, each, the liquid-fire column rising. For the giving of body's liquid gift is the giving of energy. And the lover says, "I am opened by this gift. I am open and filled." Two clasped together in the moment. Light giving. Holy. Orgasm. Two flutes play. Two bodies are the columns in front of the holy temple. Touch is the sacred pathway. Orgasm opens the doors to the most holy place. In this temple of prayer-sighs. Which temple? The temple of the void. The temple of that which ever is, of that from which all things arise. Darkness eternal. Black goddess. Creatrix. In orgasm, two doors open to the sacred place. The body, in that moment when doors swing open, is flooded with the energy of timelessness, of pure beingness. One returns to the source. Two return to the source. There they are transformed, there bathed in nothingness. In no-time's water. From there they emerge pure, emerge cleansed, emerge open to the wholeness. Know this! Know what sacredness your body contains. What avenue to sacredness the body is capable of being. Two flutes play. And the portals swing open. Briefly open. For a glimpse of the nothingness. The void. Which is, makes, contains all things. Bow down to this, revere this. And carry new torches away, when the senses are open again. New light, new flesh. Beings, cleansed. For there is joy in this. A weaving of the eternal. This is the sacrament of flesh. This is union.

Sit quietly, two together. Reach out light filled hands and feel each other's energy. Feel fire. Feel water. Meditate on the body, on the body's gifts. Meditate on the opening of spirit. From where I am, flesh is no barrier. I live in a body of light. We live, here, in bodies of light. We share, we love, we mingle. But what we know here we learned through the limits of incarnation. What we know here, lives in balance. Love is balanced. Men loving men. Women loving women. Men and women loving. Each loving the All. Each loving the self. It is no easy task to love like this, in spirit. But the flute player's love is a teaching. The flute player's love prepares. And as you play, you dance, you find union with the cosmos. And you carry to the planet the special needed vibrations that only you can share. So in the face of anger, of incomprehension, remember that the sacred holy love of men for men is needed. For it opens, connects, unites. In a world of many differences, all create a web of light. And you must, and you must share your light.

And you will set up your encampments. Your tents of flute playing lovers. And there will burn before them vast pillars of liquid-fire. Columns of love. Transmitters. Receivers. Of divinity.

This is not just sex you engage in. This is the answer to your loneliness and fears. This is an opening to communication. On your plane and others. For where I speak and share wisdom, others speak. Who know, who remember, who foresee. The chain, the sphere of man's love history. Now you still carry the pain of ten thousand years. Begin to say, "Play flute with me." Say that, begin there. And the joy will follow. My joy. Our joy. And the blessings.

I am not the only one speaking. Others are speaking. And beyond us there is Spirit speaking. The Spirit of man-love. Echoing. Echoing. If you listen. Within. Beyond the shapes and words you know.

One flute plays. Two flutes play. A circle of flutes play. The world is changed. Not by force. Force only turns stones. No, let the weight of stones be transmuted, sculpted, changed by spirit.

I wait, and others wait. The history of men loving men, both past and future, waits. Where two men love, they beckon, they carry that history. Dance in it, sing in it, sing it out loudly. Summon the saints and the heroes. For we on the other side, we are anxious to speak, to share our greater vision. We are anxious to share our timelessness. We are you, yourselves, transmuted.

Listen
listen
listen
somewhere
in the stillness
flutes play
sweetly

All through the ages there have been gay men. Though never a word existed. Though many were celibate or married. It is the loving that has always existed. Since time began. For our tribe is ancient, and we carry its history. Both the love and the torturous pain. So let us remember the loving, and use the pain as a lever in our transformation.

Two who love will glow and be splendid. History has not allowed us this splendor. It has been stifled, turned inward. But now is the time to release it. Now, as the world changes. For without you releasing your loving, without everyone doing this, you will destroy yourselves, destroy the planet. You are afraid of reprisals, and I say the world is changing. Some fear is present fear, in yourselves. But much fear comes from the memory of the inquisitions of the past. Step out, come out, into a new day. When you step out, come out, you make a change for everyone.

People say, "Why this struggle? If this path is good, why is it so difficult?" And I remind you that we have been tortured for centuries. We carry this history with us. And while other people have been hated, tortured, they had their communities, they lived and died together. We have died alone. It has been thousands of years since gay tribes wandered this planet. But there were such tribes, and there will be such tribes again. Men leaving the groups they were born in. Men traveling from place to place. Men joined together by a common language. Men of all tribes. Carrying news, music, magic, from place to place. Helping to bind the world together. This is our past/future vision. Our desire. A necessity.

And how does it begin? It begins in a small way. Two flutes play. Men hear their shared music. Coming from deep, from ancient places. Two, hand in hand. Two, radiant. Two, ancient. Around them music gathers, circuits open, energy flows. In the electric space between them. Vibrant, shared. Creating joy. In the space between two faces. In the music path the eyes create. Brain-halves crossing through the eyes. Opening lovers' brain halves. Two halves opening to the other. And to the self. Brain halves functioning together. Electric. United. Open. No longer halved.

Opening Old Gates

You measure civilizations by their remains, as if what is left can tell you how it was to be alive then. You turn to literature, you look at art, you measure beauty and say, This was a high culture, here they were experiencing a renaissance of culture. But I say, What of the things you cannot see, what of the aspects of life that do not remain? You turn to ancient Egypt, to Greece, to Italy, and fill yourself with artful dreams. But I say, There were times in your history when civilization was total, and real. People suffered and starved while Renaissance painters mimicked the world of fullness to perfection on flat surfaces. But what of the true human life of perfection, what of the ideal of happiness? Who dreams the grandest dreams, who paints them the largest, is that one the most happy?

I will tell you of another time, another way. Of a great civilization to which all of you are heirs. A civilization however that left few remains. Here a knife, there a picture, here a bone carved, there a cave discovered. A cold, a distant civilization. One that hovered on the edge of Europe's ice age. When half the continent still slept beneath its glaciers, when one could still move easily from Europe to Africa. I will tell you of that time and place. For all your dreams of perfection, of classical Greece, eternal Egypt, your balmy white-robed Atlantis dreams, and your inscrutable sense that happiness and fullness and freedom are real and can exist, in a world of chaotic changes, those ideas are memories of that distant place. And you turn the cloaks of fur to silks, the heavy boots to sandals, you call the feeling of inner warmth by its outer face. But each time one of you stops and sighs and says, "Why does it have to be this way?"—the memory of the ice age has stirred in you. The mind is about to remember.

You measure your civilizations by their remains. A poem, a potsherd, a ring, a foundation. You divide your human world into history and prehistory. You divide cultures into primitive and civilized. So I want to tell you of a time when humans lived nomadically, in tents, in caves, in temporary villages, whose houses were built of trees and reeds on piles that could be abandoned at the end of a season. This was a culture that did not have the wheel, although it had fire. It had no written language, no king, no leaders. To the outer eye those people would be called primitive. But to the inner seeing eye theirs was a culture of extreme sophistication. A tribe whose children by the age of three had already memorized vast song cycles, whose recitation around a camp fire took the night hours of three weeks to tell. A people so well attuned to nature that weather changes, earthquakes, floods were all known in advance, by smell, by hearing, by the feel beneath one's feet. This was a time when people would heal by singing, by manipulating the body's healing process through sound alone. But a time when people were rarely ill, who lived full lifetimes under adverse conditions. Whose moment of death was freely and consciously chosen. A people who lived and loved and worked in tribes. Where people of common affinity bonded together. Where no interest or desire was stifled. A people who lacked the word for war in their language. Whose powers of mind-connection were so advanced that they were in contact with unseen people half a world away. Talking and sharing their perceptions. And you say, "How nice a world you made up." And I say, not made up. I remember.

You find it acceptable to believe in saints, in great teachers of the past, in enlightened beings. But then you keep them "out there," in the distance, flat as a picture, lifeless, without thinking how active we still are, how vital, how deep a source of comfort we can be and also a source of constant information. Some of us are known, others unknown. All of us waiting to help, guide, love.

My name is Yamati. I was born in a village in what is now the south of France, in a year you would call 9098 B.C. My parents were of the tribe of artisans, craftspeople. "As a bird flies," my mother used to say, "so do we weave." We had no word in our language for "tree." We called each by its own name. Nor did we think all people were the same. The diversity of all was respected, expected. And part of the process of growing up was to seek the clan or tribe of your own affinity. This may not be the picture you have of tribal existence, where children follow their parents, on and on, generation after generation. We were not primitive. Our language for example had 32 ways to say "be," depending on age, experience, situation, time, and included the relation to the speaker. So we had fisher tribes, healing tribes, storytelling tribes, clothing-making tribes. We had people who raised children and people who didn't. We had priestess and priest clans. We had many tribes of gay people.

To hear that may sound strange to you, "tribes of gay people." First remember that the tribe of your birth was seldom the tribe of your adulthood. What your parents did was not necessarily what you yourself did. We had no division of labor by sex, we had division of labor according to interest. If you wanted to be a weaver, you joined the weaver tribe. And something in the nature of people was such that not everyone wanted to be a weaver. And if by chance it happened that more young people sought the weaving clan than in times past, it surely followed in the future that there would be extra need for nets, ropes and cloth. So we had weavers, and hunters, and gatherers, and gay people living in groups.

Let me explain that we had no marriage as you know it. We had no ceremony, no public rites. Our people did mate, did live together, and this mating was usually for life. But it came after a period of sexual randomness, and it did not preclude sexual activity, in addition to the mate relationship, in ceremonies at the equinoxes and at certain full moons. So we generally paired for life, but from the beginning men and women paired with their own sex as often as with the other. What was important to us in a relationship was how two together could aid and enhance each other's work. So that part of mating was finding someone in your own tribe to work with, and came at a time when you had found your tribe. And be it woman or man, that didn't matter. What mattered to us was the *churra*, what you would call the resonance, the spiritual harmony. Love we saw as a way to keep the work-fires burning.

We had many saints, many heroes, both female and male, but I want to speak here of the saints and heroes of the gay tribes. For this is a period of human history that has been lost through time, whose return is vitally needed. For you know the heroes of the other tribes. But of this small, sacred tribe, whose history has been obscured, you remember nothing.

Tayarti, who lived long before my time, was the greatest saint of the gay tribes. He was our christ, our buddha, our benefactor and our channel to Spirit. I leave it to others to tell the tales of the lesbian tribes, and the story of Nazimadriad, the greatest of the lesbian saints of our era. Tayarti did not discover gayness. Men have loved men since the beginning of time. And up till the end of our era there were men who loved men, who lived with the hunter or carver or arrow-maker tribes. But it was Tayarti who first, in the caves, in the cold, at the edge of the dancing grounds, would gather about him other gay men, to teach and to chant. For he saw that in his time a new healing was needed. And he saw that the power of that healing had existed all along, in the love, in the mate-bonds, in the sharing that exists between two men.

It was Tayarti who gathered about him the first gay tribe. Not all gay men came to him. Only those men came who heard the call. And the call was spirit. And the call was about holding the people together. For the great thaw was beginning. And for the first time in ages beyond remembering, there were plants to eat, and fish and other animals. And as the cold lessened, as people began to move apart, new illnesses appeared, and new hostilities. Tayarti could see in his heart that the love of his people as they traveled from village to village and from tribe to tribe, that the love of his people could speak to the whole people, could hold them together as one great tribe. For the old ways were breaking down.

As the ice receded there was more room to travel, more room for plant-ing, and people felt the desire to settle down. As people began to live in permanent villages beside their fields, the old tribal structure fell apart. When everyone moved, it didn't matter who you moved with. Hunters went off to hunt the larger animals, potters went off to the clay fields, fishers went to their streams. We all moved with our tribes, and we all returned to the central meeting grounds eight times a year, to visit, to dance, to sing, to exchange our goods and food. But as more and more people began to settle down, as ground needed to be broken and planted and tended, it was no longer easy for children to wander off, seeking the tribe of their own affinity. No, with connection to the land, marriage began, possession began to be locked into ownership. Tayarti saw frustrations growing, with the new freedom that the end of the ice allowed. Without the constant struggle against the weather, in spite of the ease and the joy of new discovery, there was no sure way to heal the wounds as there had been in the past. Tayarti saw the problem, and he saw amongst his men a certain kind of energy, a pure, direct kind of healing.

As we began to eat more plants, to cultivate plants, we needed a medicine to cleanse and to balance. Tayarti found the healing plants. Everyone knew that, the villagers and the tribespeople. Although Tayarti was a gay man, he was a hero to everyone. There was no prejudice, no hatred. Tayarti was seen as a savior, one of many saviors, one of many men, and women, coming from all different places and tribes amongst the people of the connected world that surrounded the Mediterranean. He was one of many born to be a bridge between the old and the new ways. All hailed his healing, women and men, as the gay tribes hailed also the healing of straight people. But Tayarti was, and is and always will be our most special saint. For wherever two men love, the blessing of Tayarti is there.

Tayarti was born in Kamuza, a tiny encampment at the foot of the Pyrenees. He was the third child, the first son. His father and mother were of the elk-hunter tribe, who roamed far away from the rest of the tribes, following the elk herd. Tayarti knew the mountain passageways. He knew the silence of a hunter waiting. He knew the prayer to the spirits: "Preserve me by this needed killing. I take what I take in holiness to make holiness." He knew the prayer that hunters would make as their spears and arrows shot for the mark. He and his sisters learned early to smell the smell of elk on trees, on air, to know the elk ways, as they traveled with two other families. They set up their camp fires, huddled in caves, sang their night songs. And it was the son of one of those other two families, Numitti, who became Tayarti's mate.

The two of them hunted the elk together. They prayed together and they danced. Sharing their bed furs, sharing their night dreams. Traveling with the families, with the other women and men who came to see what the elk hunt was like, to join perhaps the elk hunters tribe. It was only after Numitti's death, when Tayarti was thirty-seven, that Numitti came to him in a dream, telling him to gather about him men who love men, to heal. It was only then that Tayarti began to travel. Moving from village to village to village. Spreading his message, gathering men to his side. And he would teach them new dances, that came to him in visions, and he would teach them the roots and the healing plants. And they would wander from encampment to encampment, from village to village. Gathering here and there men who heard the calling.

Tayarti had eyes of piercing grey, cold as the night, and hot as the unseen edge of fire. And even in his old age he was beautiful. Surrounded by his big black wolf-dogs. White beard flowing beneath those piercing eyes. And if someone stared deeply into you, you said, "Does Tayarti look out?" And we called the star Sirius, Tayarti's star. And we told again and again the story of his life and his death. How he was born into the elk-hunter tribe, and mated with a man named Numitti. And how after Numitti's death the call came to Tayarti to teach and to heal. So he gathered around himself men who loved men, men whom he taught the healing of rocks and plants and chanting. Men with whom he traveled from camp to camp, from tribe to tribe, healing. Men who went out in pairs, in groups, to do their healing. And he stayed through moon after moon with his men. And it came in the year when he was 80, and a very, very old man among our people, that the longest night of the year was also a full moon night. And Tayarti gathered all his men around him. And they stamped out and cleared out a huge dancing ground. And they danced and sang all night, Tayarti's tribe. Danced and sang around a huge fire. And the cold did not touch them. For they knew the ways of making the body immune to cold by deep breathing. So they sang and they danced. Men, lovers of men. And while the night faded, Tayarti left them. And he began his climb away, up the foot of the mountain beneath which his followers danced. And as the sun rose, someone noticed that he had left them. And they began to follow him. And he turned, and he stretched out his hands to still and to bless them. And they understood then, and they did not follow him. As he climbed, he became a speck against the snow. Only a small red dot, in the red-dyed fur cloak. First a dot, and then nothing, against the whiteness.

When he was gone, his men remembered what he had said. "One day, when I am dead, I will be with you all the time." And so it began, that his men taught Tayarti's healings. And in the villages and in the tribes of the people were born other men who would seek out their teachings, their healings. And in their search, in their call, in their quest, they called out to Tayarti, and he answered them. In the ways that he led them. And we prayed to him always. "Tayarti. Teacher, healer, always present. Come speak to me, heal me, give me the great gift of healing." And such was Tayarti, our teacher, our father, our saint.

Of his healing, let me say this. That our tribes were composed as much of the dead as of the living. That those who had children were the guardians of the future, while those of us who were childless were seen to be the guardians of the past. We were the ones who spoke to the dead after they passed beyond the flesh. We were the ones who passed on advice from the dead. For the dead were known to us as the children of the spirit. They were not seen as gone from us, but only changed. And when the ice began to thaw, and people began to settle on their own lands, it was Tayarti who saw the links to the past being severed. And it was Tayarti who taught his students how to talk to the ones who passed beyond the flesh. For there were tribes of humans who had for hundreds of thousands of years lived the old ways. But Tayarti saw that the old tribal ways would break down. So slowly that even in your time this new way is still just emerging piece by piece. For millions of years there were free moving tribes. And the history of your landed world as you know it is only a few thousand years long. So we hail Tayarti, who helped prepare for this new way. We are blessed by Tayarti. Whose memory heals. Whose name heals in the changing.

We had other heroes, other saints, in those days. If Tayarti was our avatar, our ideal, Mayurdani and Namukra were our folk heroes, our life models, our play friends. They were courageous, they were saintly, but above all, they were funny. They were our Nasrudin, our wise men of Chelm, they were our Marx brothers, all rolled into two. By our stories of Mayurdani and Namukra we learned, we saw, we laughed. That they were real men, of that we had no doubt. But around their real remembered history there grew up the tales which always began with "There was a time when Namukra and Mayurdani were . . ." So let me tell you one of them.

There was a time when Mayurdani and Namukra were crossing an ice flow that stretched between the village of the deer-skin scrapers and the permanent encampment of the nut-paste-making women. Now it was hot (for the time) and Namukra was wearing his cloak unfastened. As he walked, little by little, the cloak would fall off his shoulders, and Mayurdani, who walked behind him, pulling the sledge that carried their tent and their herbs, would call out "My beloved, your cloak is slipping!" So Namukra would pull the fur cloak up around his shoulders, whistling. But as he walked, again and again the cloak would slip. So the day went by like this, with Mayurdani calling out over and over again, till he was finally tired of this, stopped, and yelled out to Namukra, "Once and for all, either tie up your cloak or pack it away. I am tired of seeing it slip, about to drop. I am tired of knowing the cold will come as sure as nightfall, and you, left to your own resources, you, so oblivious, will have long ago lost your cloak, and will be searching here, there, all over in the snow. Under your feet, all around you, searching for a spot half a day removed from where you are." So Namukra pulled the neck cords of his cloak tight, as if noticing them for the first time. He pulled the cloak strings tight and said to his beloved, "Oh my mate, how blessed I am to be followed by you. For you, Mayurdani, so wise as you are, you see my every fault. You see them all. All day long. Over and over again. You see each little fault of mine, even before I make one."

Let me tell you another story. There was a time when Mayurdani and Namukra were sitting in the mouth of a cave, preparing a fire, upon which they intended to roast a rabbit they had trapped. Now the wind was blowing into the cave, a very small cave, in such a way that whenever Mayurdani hit stone on stone and caught the sparks in dried up leaves and fanned the tiny flame, whenever he got a bit of fire going, the wind would rush in and blow the fire out. At first Mayurdani grew angry and he fanned the fire furiously, hitting for sparks in cupped hands, while Namukra fanned the flame. But again and again the wind would blow the fire out.

At first he was angry, and then his anger changed to reason, and he turned to Namukra and he said, "Look, my mate, I have an idea. If we pile up stones in the entrance to the cave, the wind will not be able to blow through, and we can build a fire upon which to roast our meat." Namukra said, "How wise you are Mayurdani. All along I knew you would find a way to solve our problem." And Namukra left the cave, climbing down the rock, and he returned with an armful of stones, which he spread out in the entrance to the cave. Meanwhile, With his back to the wind, Namukra formed a wind break with his cloak, which Mayurdani did not see, as he made sparks till the fire caught, vaguely shielded by the tiny wall of stones that he thought was cutting the wind.

Children laughed at these stories of foolishness. And the youths of Tayarti's tribe would ponder their hidden meaning. For what part of us is Mayurdani, what part Namukra, what is the wind, what the cave, what the fire? And when do we put our back to a problem, instead of facing it head on, in order to solve it? We laughed at these two. At Mayurdani who thought himself so wise, and at Namukra who thought himself so foolish. We laughed, but we lived like them also. For side by side with the funny stories were the tender stories. Of how Mayurdani courted Namukra. Namukra who was so busy singing to the Mother that he did not notice the man who sat beside him day after day. Who only gradually came out of his spirit-filled trance to see beside him a man of unearthly beauty, beating the drum that had deepened him and kept him from getting lost in his trance.

It is said that Mayurdani beat the drum for Namukra for two days without stop, for three days, and a fourth, wanting him, aching for him, in love with the beauty of his grace. And with each drumbeat it was Namukra he sought to reach. And at the end, Namukra emerged from his trance and saw beside him a green-eyed man of such beauty that the whole song tribe fell silent whenever he danced. Namukra saw the beauty of the man who had kept him company, who had paced his deepening of song. Namukra finally saw Mayurdani and reached out to him, reached out a numb, half frozen hand. And Mayurdani loved him so well for the god-song in him that he began to beat the drum again. And they went on like that for day after day after day, so deep in trance that they did not sleep or eat. And they would have made god-circles of their music for so long that their spirits would have left their flesh. But the drum skin burst at last. And Namukra fell, transfixed into Mayurdani's swollen arms. And so, it is said, they began their life together. Too numb to touch. So spirit-filled, they did not have to.

In those days amongst our tribe, we had the gifts of inner speech so well developed that two lovers could speak to each other at a distance, and our wise men could speak to the wise ones of cultures in Tibet, Africa, and the Americas. So you see, our world was in no way small or isolated. For even then, even more so than today, all branches of the human race were united. So Namukra and Mayurdani were united by the special strength of their inner speaking. For love makes the inner voice speak. And there was no place in one, no hurt, no joy, no pain, that was not shared by the other.

It is said that on a certain spring day, Mayurdani was visiting the village of his grandparents, and Namukra was sitting in a field ten miles away. The two of them were arguing about the nature of the universe, debating at that distance with inner talk, inner fight in that case. Namukra said that the universe went on forever. Mayurdani was adamant about its limits. Namukra said it had no beginning in time, so how could it have an end in space. For if it had an end, didn't it have to be within something else? And if it was within something else, wasn't that an object itself, which would have to have an end somewhere? But Mayurdani said that surely as smoke fades into air, that the universe faded out, thinned out. And their debate was so intense, even at the distance of ten miles, that when a wild beast came roaring into the clearing where Namukra sat, came racing through the underbrush, Namukra ignored it, to continue his point. And when it charged, he turned to it as if to say, "Please, can't you see that I'm talking. I have no time for this." And when it charged, and when it gored him, and when it severed the connection between his body and his spirit, Namukra paused for a moment to gather his senses, in that other place, thanked the beast for helping him, and turned back to Mayurdani saying, "I told you. I was right. It is endless!"

Even in death they were united. And when from loneliness of the flesh, Mayurdani chose to end his earthly existence two years later, having done all the dancing he could and all the teaching, Namukra was there beside him, waiting. And they are together always, who were children in the days of Tayarti, who remembered him, who carried on his teachings, who teach still as we remember them.

Of another great teacher I will speak. Of Akidrada, the eastern sage of our people. Who was born in what was called Nah-ruth, today the north of Italy. Akidrada lived in the days when the landed people were establishing themselves. when men were carving up the world into plots and pieces and little kingdoms. He lived in the days when free women were giving up their power in the name of land, protection, and inheritance for their children, which seemed a good idea at the time. Now the tribe of Tayarti was already fallen under suspicion, although their healing and their wisdom were still welcome by the landed people. They were met with suspicion, not yet for being gay but because they moved from place to place. For free movement, once the life of all the people, was coming to be feared, the work of enemies. invaders or spies. No, the ice was gone, the world had changed. In the comfort of warmth. the spiritual gifts were being forgotten. As in your day, in the midst of another kind of ice, another kind of death, they are being remembered again.

Akidrada was born in those days. The shining light of the gay peoples. Our last great sage. Love was his message as it had been of every teacher before him. Love was his message. In the days when greed began its fearsome reign. Love was his message and he wandered from village to village. And he looked for his own people, he looked for the gay men. And wherever they were, he came and he loved them. He shared their pallets, and he taught the sacrament of Tayarti. Where touch leads to the deepening. the opening. of the flesh. Where in orgasm the body becomes an opening to the flow of holy spirit. Akidrada taught love that way. And whoever was loved by him could not ever be the same. No, his soul was imprinted with that sacred gift. Imprinted down, down, down through the ages. Imprinted in life after life, incarnation after incarnation. And the blessing of his love has carried gay men through torture and pain, through fiery deaths, through rage, through self-hatred. For he stamped by his embraces the love of the ages. He passed it to his lovers. And he left them to pass it on again. And then there came a day when he touched no more, but only sang. And his songs were as powerful as his touch was. And so I repeat his words as I heard them in my youth.

Ayuta, ayuta, nahiid
Ayuta, ayuta, naharida
Ayuta, pohanaya naharid
Ayuta, ayuta, ayudi.
Come love, come love, bless me
Come love, come love, drink blessing
Come love, drop into silent dark blessing
Come love, come love, let us be lovers.

Tayarti was the opening, Mayurdani and Namukra were the fullness, and Akidrada was the seal. These are our saints. These are our patrons. Each one a blessing. Each one a path. When Akidrada sang of Tayarti, grown men cried in bliss. For what he felt in his heart, he gave to them.

So sing again, gay people. Lift up your voices in song and dance. For what was once, shall be again. And we shall touch, we shall love, we shall heal again.

So sing again, gay peoples. Sing. Raise up your voices to the sky. Raise up your voices so the earth can hear you. Remember the ones who sang before you, and sing again.

Deepening Into the Man-Womb

Each man carries in his heart a place, a womb-nest, a silent fifth chamber. One that does not pump, but waits. One that does not send forth, but receives. And the heart of the man-womb is a nesting. And in the nesting is the presence of Love, of the child Love. Born everywhere, born in the hearts of all men who love men. Nurtured in the hearts of all men by their loving. This presence of Love is the self-seed. All who seek to find true meaning need turn inward only, and meditate on Love's presence. A flame's spark in the hearts of all men who love men. Fanned by their loving. Mirrored in their loving. Echoed. Multiplied. Blessed. And who grows in his loving, within him grows his Love. "You are strong of Love," we would say. "Love is full in him." So that we were all Love, we all became Love. The flute players. The men of the woods. The song-healers. Opening. Opening. Opening.

Sit quietly. Feel the press of air upon your skin. Feel the outward press of body breathing. Feel your consciousness glowing in your head. Feel it glow. Feel it grow heavy. And now feel it, make it drop. Slowly. Drop deep into your heart. Drop deep with its glowing. Drop deep into the heart. Drop deep. To illuminate the man-womb.

What man gives man is born in the heart. What is born in the hearts of men is Love. Feel the warmth of light drop into your heart. See it illuminate the waiting place. See it illuminate the tiny presence of Love there. Focus on that tiny figure, that tiny child. See it, feel it warm inside. Now, begin to make it grow. See it grow beyond the borders of your heart. Feel it grow. Feel it fill you. Till you and the presence of Love are the same size. Till the presence of Love within you has grown to fill your body. Till you feel yourself one with it.

Now, feel the presence grow. Feel the presence grow again, outward. Feel it grow out beyond the confines of your physical body. Feel it expand, stretch out, reach out toward the hearts of other womb-men, other lovers. Two flutes play. Two men filled with light meet. And they dance Tayarti's ancient love dance. Love meeting Love. Love meeting itself in the hearts of two men. Light in the hearts of two men glowing. Joining. Spreading. Filling the world. Blessing it.

It is the moon that rocks in the heart. It is the boat of the moon in which Love travels. Its left horn is compassion and its right horn is understanding.

Love whispers moonlight. Love remembers when the moon was male, when men were like the moon. Changing. Love, male, in the boat called moon. Rocking in your heart, with a flute in his lap. And only when a man has played flute with the presence within him can he play flute with a man of flesh. Two flutes, echoing, echoing.

Can you see the way to remember? Can you remember the way to this place? When we were one with the world. One in it. Doing our flute dance. Remembering the days when the moon was male, when the earth was male, when we saw them as male, and loved them for their craggy strength, their fluid richness. When the two of them circled and danced around each other as lovers. Can you see that? Can you remember that in yourself?

We used to hold each other. We used to comfort each other. Men in your world do not. You comfort no longer. And must relearn this. To rock, to cradle, to soothe again. You have sex with each other, or you kill each other. But you allow yourselves no touching in between. Not only you, but all men must relearn this. Teach by your doing and let them see. Let them see the strength of gentle nurturing.

Deepening into the man-womb. Deep in a cave. Wall paintings live, flickering in the light of burning oil. Small fires. Soft light, deep in the heart of the earth. Deep in the heart of flesh. For the heart is a cave. The heart remembers. Where the man-womb resides. Where the light dwells, waiting. Always waiting.

Men must believe that they can birth newness. The fruit of a man's life is this birthing. A child, a poem, a play, a harvest. All this is a birthing. Men who love men are birthing. The seeds that plant a star can be man-birthed. Ask yourself now what you have birthed in your time. See yourself now on your deathbed, old, waiting. See yourself now as the old man you will be and ask yourself what you have birthed of your life. Has it been fullness, or pain? Has it been beauty, joy or only a bitter seed of woundedness never transcended? See yourself now lying on your deathbed. Let yourself feel as well as see the man who you will become. Look at your age, your place. How does that feel to you now? To be looking back on your life, to be looking back from that bed to parts of your life you haven't lived yet. Are you proud of the life you had, proud of the things you birthed in it? Is it joy you see as you look back, or only suffering? And what of the men you have loved, and what of the friends you have cared for? Is there goodness there, or only sorrow? What do you see as you look back? What have you birthed from your man-heart?

When a man turns deep into the man-womb, the world forever changes. When he takes the glowing to heart from head, he cannot ever be the same again. And if you lay in bed night after night in wondering, do not wonder any more. Just close your eyes and see yourself so small that you can sit in the middle of your brain, that you can see yourself begin to walk. From head, turn south, set out for the heart, for the man-womb. This is the purest journey you can make. Watch for signs along the way. Watch the branching of streams and rivers. This is your inner landscape. This is your own special place. And you will make it to the man-womb if you keep on walking. No man fails who seeks to find this place. And the light within is a blessing. A blessing to be carried back to the brain. A blessing to be given to the world. This is your night's meditation. The pathway. The doorway. Your sacred entry place.

When you set out on this journey you will meet friends along the way. You will meet teachers and other seekers. The whole of gay history you can meet along the way. For what is born in the man-womb lives on forever. Nothing lost, all remembered, all saved. All joy, present. All pain, present. Nothing lost, all men saved. Deepening into the man-womb. Deep. Bearing place. New birthing man place.

The spark of man love quickens in the man-womb. What two men quicken in each other, falls as a light rain of love upon the world. Deepening into the man-womb, they travel outward. Deepening into the man-womb, they find eternity.

What will be seen again has not been seen these ten thousand years. The root of it was planted then. But what will be seen among men has never been seen before. Root planted, growing silently, bears fruit today. "Caress me, beloved," I cried out then. And now, ten thousand years later, I see a world about to happen where men can answer me.

The sacred places of the recent past were shrines and temples. They were built on the labor of human backs. But I say that today, the sacred places of the world are to be found within. And your pilgrimages will be inward. Carrying visions of the outer world, but finding it within you. Finding the holy place deep within. For as a shrine or a temple is sacred, so must the body be. Be shrine for the light of Loving. Teach this to your children. Teach them to sit in silence, teach them to know the subtle path inward. For what one sees in the self when one sees it in the body, can be seen in all others, be seen in all people. So your healings will change. And your world will change.

No more violence, no more rape, no more killing. And you laugh or sigh and say, "How can this happen?" And I answer, Where two flutes play, they play music from the world of pure spirit. Even in silence, unseen by the world. Such love breeds change. So dare to love. Your love is a broadcast system. For what began to change in my age from harmony to chaos, now turns more than ten thousand years later from chaos to the beginning of harmony. What began in harmony, the shift of divine images, the change in sex-roles and relation to the Earth itself, what began in hierarchical thinking, transmutes in your age at last to a new equality, a new relation to each other and to the globe. And in this new era of history, we forgotten ancestors will be remembered again.

In our era, we had no chieftains, no kings, no leaders. We trusted in the greater whole of all people, and from birth were taught to express our unique-ness—and so in the future shall you. In the revolutionary rumblings of two centuries ago your future began. And if at this moment it seems impossibly remote to you, remember that I and others like myself are speaking because like attracts like; and we are drawn to your new sense of freedom.

So we traveled, we wandered, we moved in pairs, in bands. We did our healing when it needed to be done. Two lovers, two flute players, two gath-erers of herbs, and chanters of chants. Woven deep, deep into the man-womb of each, drawing forth from that magic place the power to heal the sick. Two lovers can do this. Any two lovers can do this. Sit at head and foot, or on either side of a person unwell. Draw forth in their minds the light that lives deep in the heart. Draw it forth and cast it, each into the heart of each, like fishermen at sea, casting their love-breath deeper and deeper, casting a web about the sick one. Raising the sick one up from the depths. On the strength of their shared love. On the beauty. Of man mirroring man. Of god-self, reflected. Of twin beloveds nurturing their friend. This is the hidden power of gay love. Deep as the heart, far greater than the slick skill of physicians.

Healing is the child of man love. Tayarti felt this. He left it as his gift. To a humanity that is tearing itself away from its roots. That needs to weave itself back again, into wholeness again. Tayarti saw the gift that man-loving men carried deep in their hearts. A different kind of healing web. Different than women's healing, different and yet the same. All of them different heal-ing webs. But this is Tayarti's web. A gift from the end of the ice ages. A gift to the men of this century.

Let two men sit, night after night, by candle, in darkness. Let two men sit, face to face, who love, who share life together. Let two men sit quietly, in silence. Feeling each the warmth, the light of heart. Sit till you feel it. Sit till you feel it move from breast to breast. Send it directly, send it in circles. Fill in the space between you with this radiance. Chant as you do this. Let your sounds augment the light-passage. Pass love as you do this. Love is light-energy traveling. Fill up the spaces between you as you do this. Experiment. Move closer, move further apart. Feel how distant you can move and yet still feel the flow of light connect you. This is the healing gift starting to mani-fest. Believe in it. Believe that what you vision-see, what you imagine you "see," is real.

Deepening, deepening in the night. Deep into the darkness. Flesh body of man, with its visceral knots and cerebral spiraling. Hung on the elegant symmetrical lines and flows of the electrical body. Deep in him. Deep in the man. Deep in him, glowing. And the mind of light, the voice of light, the heart of light, the stomach of light, the man-womb, endlessly glowing. The man-womb, organ, unsung, unpraised. Love is deepening, dropping down into the man-womb. Whose product, whose child, is not flesh, not art, but eternal renewal of self. So a man deepens. In sleep, in tenderness. Each touch deepens. As warm hand melts ice and sinks deep in it. So love deepens, love reaches the man-womb. Glorious. Light-filled. Renewing.

In our caves we sang of the man-womb, of the source, of the glowing creative place. In our caves we sang. And I tell of the day when man-loving-man love will once again teach. When from city to city, from town, from ruin, the loving men tribe will move out. Move out into the world, carrying this healing. Singing, two by two, in groups. Men wandering. And when the fires die down, they will speak. Of the man-womb. Of self nurturing. Men who love men will know this. And when all people know and understand this, then the race of humans will be free again. Spiraling, deepening. What was past reemerges, changed, new, cleansed. And the men who love men return, renewed, cleansed. Tree-tall and earth-still. Spiraling. Elegant.

"Touch me," a man says to his lover. "Touch me with hands of light. Open my man-womb." And the lover stretches glowing hands out. And his hands are a kiss. His touch a benediction. As he touches the man he loves. And the body of the man he loves becomes light. And in the heart of his man-womb is a child of light. And the light is Pure Spirit. The light is Truth. The light is Love.

Love is a gift of hands, not eyes. Love is a gift of hands that heal. And healing is a gift of light. Men who sit, men who take the time to sit and feel the light inside, have the gift of hands alive in them to give. They have the gift of love inside. To feel the light, the love, is simply to imagine it. For imagination is deeper seeing that your culture has denied. So imagine that your hands are giving out light from the palm and the end of each finger, and what you are imagining is what is really there. And the source of the light is in the heart. In the fifth chamber of the heart, in the man-womb. So imagine that you feel the light in the center of your heart. And what you imagine is what is real. That you have not felt before. That you have not been taught that you can feel. That you felt as a child, and were taught to forget in order to grow up. But I say, grow down! Grow down in the body, grow down into the heart. And feel the Earth feed your heart, sending its own light up through your feet. And let the heavens feed your heart, sending its light down through the top of your head, into the heart. And let love feed your heart. And with your heart, feed the hearts of those you love. Till all men glow with the inner heart-light of man love.

The body of man is a tree of light, a column of light, pouring out from the heart. Be an oak, be a beacon, be a tower of love in the world. Share your light, share your loving. Stand face to face, lay body to body. Share your light, share your love with another. Man-womb pressed to man-womb. Light pressed to light, glowing and mingling. Be flute players. Pour out your light in song. Dare to be the light-bearer you always dream you are.

All through the ages, men have loved men. Long before the ice, in the warmth of the earliest human world, men loved men. Such love is pure, such love is ancient, such love is a necessary part of the human song. Without it, humanity cannot go on. Without it humanity is dead to its fullness, lacks the resonance that makes for life. Yes, without the man-loving-man song in the air, no human child can be born. No heir to the vast fortune of beauty and wisdom our humanness has created for itself. We knew this before. You will know this again. That same-sex loving is the cross fibering on the loom of humanness. That without it, no weaving can happen. That without it, humanity cannot exist. For same-sex loving holds the cross fibers, the cross song. For same-sex loving is the other half that makes a whole be more than itself.

We were the flute players, we healed with our hands and our music. You are healers still, blocked in your power, denied it. But the door to the light is present in the body. The man-womb is the door to light. And love is the opening of the door. If you love, if you have loved, if you have been loved, if you can feel the dream of love inside you, then the door is open. It takes no more than the dream of love to set the heart to glowing. And in the glowing is the light of your power. And our power to heal is needed more than ever now. As the world humanity has created stands on the brink of destroying itself.

You think I speak in metaphor when I use the word light. But I do not. I speak of a light that most eyes cannot see, which is as present in the world as the atom was in all the years before it was "discovered." I speak of the energy that can be perceived with practice. Whose use can be learned as can any new skill. There is nothing spiritual or mysterious about this. No more mysterious than an apple to an Eskimo, or a rainbow to a fish. No more mysterious than the love of men to those who know it. As simple and possible and real.

History has been rich with forgotten teachers, forgotten lovers. History can be rediscovered. Whatever has been, still is. Whatever has been felt, presses still against the common human mind. Whatever has been known, is knowable still. My life, the lives of other gay teachers, can be felt, remembered, understood again. So that what was anciently true about men loving men is true again. So that you know that what I say about the light, about the giving of light, the sharing of light, the chamber of light in the hearts of men, that all of this is true. And that we who are "dead" reach out to you. Saints, teachers, guides. We offer you the comfort of our lives, our wisdom, our mistakes, and our loving. For time holds in its heart the memory of any man's love for another. Holds it and cherishes it. Preserves it, as leaf pressed between the pages of Time's thickest book.

And I stop where I started. Deep in the timeless man-womb place. It is dark. All is silent. Yet as I play my flute, I hear another flute play. And I reach out with my song. And one hears me. We meet. Our songs embrace. So bend ear, delight in the songs we sing. As I draw him in spirit, draw him near to me. Each note of my song a line of words that he puts on paper. For I, Yamati, dead these years, I reach out through him, through time. And two flutes play. Water pours over itself, in the confluence of time. Two flutes play. We meet, in the deep man-womb sharing of mind. Two flutes play. They play here. They play elsewhere. Flutes play. They play of your blessedness.

Part Two:
Spiritual Love/
Sacred Sex

AIDS and Global Consciousness

AIDS is a planetary experiment. The participants on the planet range from viruses to the living being that is the planet itself. We as human beings see its focus in our lives, and it is no mistake to say that this experiment concerns us and our place on the planet.

AIDS is a planetary experiment. It is an experiment in love and compassion. It is an experiment to see whether the mass of human beings can change their consciousness levels to a point of love and understanding that embraces *all* human beings. Those who play host to this experiment may be female or male, black, brown, red, yellow or white, rich or poor—but they all have one thing in common—which may not be readily apparent on the outside—they feel that they do not belong here. As if that could be true of *anyone* who is born here. But they feel it. And in surrendering their bodies to what is often a fatal illness, they offer themselves up to this experiment, and must be applauded.

The nature of the experiment is twofold. It involves compassion and transformation on one hand. But on the other hand, it represents a doorway into one possible future for human beings on this world. If changes in consciousness do not occur, it is "possible" that in 50 years time a viral illness of such strength will appear in this world that 50 percent of all children born, will die before the age of five from diseases that make AIDS look kind. So that those who are afflicted with AIDS at this time will be seen as the voluntary vanguard in health research that will make the lives of those children involved as comfortable as possible. And even they, all those "possible" future children, will be involved in a last attempt at consciousness altering for humans on this world. If humans fail in that experiment, then human life here as you know it "may" be terminated, and you human beings relocated to other worlds, other realms, to continue your education in consciousness.

When someone completes their portion of this experiment, which most often in your current terms means to die, we who are without bodies as you know them are here to receive them and comfort them and heal them. There are certain individuals who are so involved in this experiment that they have already died two or three times, died, come back as an infant and died again—just to further the research and expand this experiment. Deadly as it seems, that "possible" future alternative will be far worse. But as soon as you see the scope of this study, you can begin to make the necessary shifts in consciousness required. If enough people do this, the consciousness airwaves will be flooded with love and compassion sufficient to alter all of human life.

The nature of a consciousness shift would be reflected in human changes that have been spoken of since the beginning of your recorded history. Freedom of identity, food, housing, clothing, education for all. Respect, the devoted parenting of children born into a world of love and inner trust. You live under the threat of global destruction by the tools of your own hands. Those tools are the results of another experiment, a playing with fire, you might call it. But if you love this world, if you love its hills and trees and blue of sky, if you love the sound of a child's laughter, the feel of someone else's skin against your skin, the taste of a fruit, the joy of a good song, then you have no choice but to change.

Change. Change. Change. It is easier to do than you think. All that you have to do is close your eyes, feel the beating of your heart. Feel the life pulsing through your body. And know that life is love. Feel that love circulates in your body. And see the people you know, friends and enemies alike. And know that love courses through their bodies too. And know that in the center of this planet, in the heart of It's own chosen body, that love pulses there too. Do this, keep doing this. Feel it, keep feeling it.

Sound is a powerful tool for healing. Align your body with the planetary axis, head in the direction of the pole that you are closest to. Close your eyes and deepen into yourself. Begin to make the highest pitched "EEE" sound that you can. Feel it pulsing through your body and traveling out your hands and feet and out the top of your head in waves that will weave into the planet itself. This will rebalance you and cleanse you.

Sight can be a useful tool. We give you a visual tool for shifting consciousness in this experiment. Copy it onto paper yourself. Make it any size that you desire. Staring at it will generate shifts in the neural patterns of your brains, to further the experiment.

Focus on the dot and keep coming back to it when your eyes wander off.

No one needs to die from AIDS. Death is not the aim of this experiment. But many have died from it and many will continue to die. People who have felt that they are outsiders may choose to die in order to learn the truth—that they are as much Earthlings as anyone else. Death is an honorable end and needs to be respected. Please make no one wrong who uses this experiment to heal themselves through death.

AIDS is a planetary experiment. It is a doorway into the future. Through it, hope and love and change can come. Through it, *because* of it! Remember that. This is an experiment in your future. No one is apart from this experiment, although some are more active participants in it. No one can say "I'm not involved. I do not have it." Everyone is involved. Everyone is a part of the experiment. Some hold the test tube, and others are in it. But no one is exempt. Nowhere on this planet is a human being exempt from this experiment. And the outcome of the experiment does not concern those few outsiders, gay, drug users, Africans. It is about a sentient world that no longer has any outsiders. It's as simple as that. And those people living in bubbles and feeling immune are as much involved as the children dying in hospital wards, or in huts in Africa.

AIDS is a planetary experiment designed to see whether or not human beings can shift their consciousness from a divisive mode to an all-embracing one. Every human being on the planet is a participant. Not just the individuals who "have" AIDS. We in subtle bodies are as much participants as you in physical form. This experiment is our chance to change human life upon this world. It's Phase One Intensified of the last chance. If you love your body, if you love the body of the being you call Earth, then there can be only one outcome—Transformation.

An incarnate species on a given planet is like a tribe unto itself. The main body of the tribe moves slowly through consciousness, while certain individuals and groups of individuals serve as consciousness scouts. They move more quickly through the terrain of awareness, seeking out areas for the body of the tribe to explore. Artists are consciousness scouts. Saints are consciousness scouts. Certain groups of people, not necessarily bound by genetic ties, serve as scouts in consciousness also. All blind people are reaching out through the perceptual terrain of sentience. Deaf people are doing the same. Handicapped people are consciousness scouts. Children and older people are also scouting out for the main body of the tribe. It is a pity that so much information is lost to you because you have forgotten about scouting. But the time is near at hand when the scouts of humanity will be honored again.

All those whose intrinsic capacity for love turns toward members of their own gender are consciousness scouts. They explore the terrain of what it means to be a woman or a man, or both. But they also have other skills as a people, as a sub-tribe, that need to be remembered and honored, by themselves and by the world.

Why has the gay community served in this country as the primary host for this experiment called AIDS? What is this experiment aiding? If it serves to aid the growth of consciousness, then it will be a very successful experiment. But if it serves only to aid fear and divisiveness, then more intense experiments in consciousness will be instituted, on a collective soul level.

The gay community in this land is participating directly in this experiment for a combination of reasons. On a body consciousness level, self-internalized rage and shame have weakened certain individuals' immune systems to the point where microscopic entities have attacked them. But those same individuals, paradoxically, have responded to something deeper in themselves, to an ancient tribal knowledge that goes back to the beginning of this era of human history.

This era of human history goes back to the end of the Ice Age. That period when the earth might have destroyed humanity served instead to deepen it in awareness. In order to survive the ice, one had to be all of who one was. People got lazy when the ice receded, spiritually lazy. So you have gone from a time when the world might have put an end to you to a time when you could put an end to it.

Gay people have specific functions that grow out of our vibratory essence. The vibratory essence of male and female are not the same. The vibratory essence of those who are drawn to their own gender in love are not the same as those who are drawn to the other gender. Gay people are healers and creators, using our energy to serve humanity. We do not have to list the great gay artists. We may have to remind you that shamans in many places were gay. But few if any will remember that for much of the Ice Ages, gay people often served as tribal midwives. Not midwives for those being born, but midwives for those who were dying. Some of the fear of gay people to this day is the lingering whiff of death and transformation unconsciously detected.

Death is not an end. There is no real death. I who write these words through another are no more dead for not having a physical body than you will be when you disconnect from yours. Death is a shift in focus. When you are dreaming, you are already a little bit dead—you are conscious without a body. Death is a shift in focus, as birth is. One takes you into physicality, the other leads you out. But to be human, fully human, is to know both. As it is equally a part of being human to have male and female lives, straight and gay lives.

In the time of the ice, gay people knew that they were attuned to helping people make the shift from physical focus to subtle body focus. Something deep within all gay people remembers this. And so the choice of participating in this planetary experiment is part of reclaiming an ancient inner skill, for the sake of the gay community, and for the healing of this world. For the whole world needs its midwives back. Supporters in birth, supporters in that transformation that you call death.

All souls rise up into incarnation through the living soul of their planet. The being you call Earth is the parent of you all. It needs its healing now, it needs its own shifts in focus. It needs you to make your own shifting, away from destroying it and back toward a time of love. You cannot love your planet if you do not love your own body. Touch yourself, hold yourself, give your own body the tenderness, the caresses you all too often wait for others to give. Touch every part of yourself. To do this is to make planetary change a little bit more possible. Deepen into the wholeness of your wisdom. And know that as more and more people become whole, that which kills now will be transformed.

AIDS is a planetary experiment, an experiment in consciousness. All human beings are involved in it, in and out of bodies. All human beings are involved in this experiment, some directly and others less directly. Those at the front line are actively working in their own ways to further planetary transformation. Some will do it through their work, others will do it through the work they inspire in others. But no one is immune, no one is not a part of this experiment. It is an experiment in love and in compassion. It is an experiment in shifting consciousness. Many out of bodies support you in your research. Together, we can all evolve in consciousness.

AIDS is a planetary experiment. If you love life, if you love your body, if you love this sparkling, shimmering being you call Earth, then there can only be one outcome to the experiment—Planetary Transformation.

Toward a Harmony
of Gender and Sexuality

The soul is genderless. Before it incarnates in a body it works to shape it from the non-physical plane. It turns on certain genes and turns off others. It makes choices about gender and sexuality, all of which are fluid. Gender is about patterns of manifestation in physical form. Sexuality is about patterns of relation. They are not the same thing. In the course of your many lives, all of you will live as women and men, all of you will live lives as same-gender lovers and other-gender lovers.

Gender is about individual information gathering. The two genders, male and female, gather information in slightly different ways. But it is a mistake to assume that sexual attraction is a quality of gender. It is not. One is not attracted to someone because of one's gender; one is attracted to someone because of their chosen sexual preference. Sexuality is about information integration between individuals. The two patterns of sexuality, same-gender loving and other-gender loving, integrate information in different ways. Love is information exchange between individuals. Many forms of love exist besides physically expressed love. Words, a hand shake, a lingering glance, a delicious conversation, all exchange information. But there is something deep and holy and energetically profound about physically expressed love, for it is the only way to exchange information on every frequency, physical and non-physical. Two men together process information differently than two women together or a woman and a man. For your species to be balanced, three patterns of information sharing are necessary.

The purpose of sexual connection is information exchange. The more profound the exchange, the deeper the love felt. The purpose of sexual connection is not primarily reproductive. There are planets where reproduction and love making do not make use of the same organs, as they do here. Species may have one set of organs for love making and another for reproducing. As you become more conscious, more aware of subtle energy, you will understand this information and come to recognize the purpose and function of love and sex in your life and in the universe. Love and sex link individuals and connect all sentient beings in a vast energetic web that ripples through physicality and has the capacity to flood it with the total joy of beingness. Passion is not love, necessarily. Sex is not love, necessarily. Love is shared resonance between two individuals that allows for soul level information exchange. Please remember that when you are searching for a love-partner. Please remember that when you are with your love-partner. Ask yourself if this is someone you want to share soul information with, if this is someone whose soul information you want to carry in your subtle fibers, whose subtle fibers you want to carry bits of yourself. As you evolve, you will come to function smoothly on all planes, and sex and love will happen harmoniously.

The harmony of gender and sex is part of human aspiration. It requires that one recognize and own one's potential to be female and male, heterosexual and homosexual. When information about the self that is contained in one's subtle fibers is repressed, the self cannot be whole, the experience of the world cannot be whole.

From the balance of female and male in each self, from the recognition of dual capacities for sexual connection in all human beings, harmony will increase in each individual and then in the world. The work that you do with yourself, the information that you share with your lovers, all can help to change the energy field of human life on this endangered planet. Each time one alone, or two together, find and share this harmony, they beam out that harmony into the world and make it a little bit easier for others to find the strength and fearlessness inside to recognize aspects of the whole self that cultures and religions have denied for so long.

In the Ice Age human beings knew about this balance, and it is time for human beings to know this about themselves again. Life, not only human life, depends upon this self-recognition. It isn't something lost or hidden, in need of being found.

All this information is contained in subtle energy circuits that wait to be turned on like light switches in darkened rooms. And we support you in this effort. You are not alone. In and out of physical bodies, all of us are human, all of us are evolving toward harmony together. Some of us have never had physical bodies, some of us are between lives, and others are done with our cycles of incarnation. Incarnate and discarnate, together we all make up Earth's sentient human community.

When you reach in to yourself for wholeness, and reach out to us for wholeness, we make together a great healing on this world, for this world. Our simple silent acts do make a difference. Quiet shifts in consciousness that happen in your mind and in your bed *do* make a difference. Please remember that. In the touch of a lover's face from the wholeness of your heart, you change the world, you make a new song echo.

The Challenges
of Spiritual Manifestation

Very early in its history an asteroid came crashing into the planet Earth, knocking it off its course, causing physical damage, and tilting it on it axis. This event disrupted the inner and outer layers of the planet, creating an instability that in order to balance itself out, ultimately resulted in the birth of what you recognize as life.

Earth is still unstable at its core, it still wobbles on its axis—in fact everything that lives upon it wobbles. To some, that is an awful tragedy, the cause of their difficulties, the source of their inability to successfully manifest spiritual intentions. For there are planets that do not wobble on their axes, do not have unstable cores. And certain individuals have lived before on such worlds, or visited them between incarnations. And when they get to Earth they often complain about the way that things are here. It does no good to tell such individuals that they have chosen to incarnate here, that no one forced them to do it. It does no good to remind such individuals that this world is one of the most varied and beautiful in this galaxy. The best that one can say to make life a bit easier is that the very factors that make Earth life difficult also make it challenging, creative and exciting. If you have lived on a planet with a stable core whose axis does not wobble you will know what I am talking about. On such worlds, spiritual life is not difficult, one does not have to struggle to learn, remember and manifest spiritual intentions on the physical plane.

But worlds like that are boring. They may not have war. But try and imagine a world where people whistle the same song for ten thousand years, and styles of clothes never change, and the same chants recited over and over again for millennia echo in the courtyards of their sacred places. That kind of life suits certain individuals. But if you are here, you can be certain that you left such a planet or checked it out and decided against it. For with all its faults, life upon the living, breathing being you call Earth is challenging and infinitely creative. The soul is stretched to its fullest capacities. And ultimately, the great difficulty is more than balanced out by the joy of Earth's diversity and infinite creative possibilities. In a single Earth year in a single city, more songs can be written and performed than on certain planets in their entire history. Please remember that.

Some people would like to stabilize the core and right the planet's axis. No matter that the planet enjoys its dance, its tilt. Some people, indeed some cultures, have set themselves up in the business of generating planetary stability. To this endeavor the Earth keeps saying, "No, just learn to dance with me." It shimmies its surface, it drums at the core. It sings and it chants. Energy lines flow and spiral and weave themselves around the planet's body in strange ways. Its continents are unsymmetrical. It storms and it rages. Such is its essence. Such is its nature. It shifts and it changes. Too fast for some, too often for many. But in its changing is growth and transformation. And those who have come knew this when they arrived here, emerged here. It is time to remember that. Time to move with it. This planet is a pearl of great price. Its irregularities are what make it so valuable. So you can resist the Earth's changing, get angry at it, or you can deepen yourself into its flesh and dance with it.

Pain, suffering, are not the result of this instability at the core. Fear of the instability is the cause of those conditions. There are more unstable worlds. Worlds with many suns and moons all tugging at them. Worlds with earthquakes and volcanos in constant motion. Worlds whose surfaces bubble endlessly like oatmeal. The beings there adjust to them eventually, move with them. It may take life after physical life. But they do it. As you shall, on your dancing planet.

If your ideal of perfection is changeless, if you imagine an Earth where things stay the same generation after generation—imagine again, for that will never happen. So too, if your goal for yourself is a state of static beingness, you need to change it. All life wobbles on this planet. Wobbles, or dances. As sometimes, when someone bumps into you on the dance floor, you turn to them with anger in your eyes. And sometimes, you turn to them and love stares back, and the bruise on your thigh was all worth it. So with Earth. It smiles, and rubs its hip.

When you understand fire, you no longer stick your hand in it, you contain it and cook with it. When you understand the wobble, you no longer fear it or hate it, you move with it, use it. And sometimes, when your life is a mess, when you've been in therapy for 57 years and you're still falling in love with the wrong person—stop blaming your parents or yourself. Stop and take a deep breath and say to yourself—"I'm living on a world that wobbles on its axis. It has seasons and changes. And sometimes, what seems to be going wrong in my life isn't really a flaw in my nature. It's just that I haven't learned to wobble with the world yet." The Earth laughs at itself. Can you? Can you feel it laughing?

Earth Ancestors

As the last of the ice receded, human consciousness had been so transformed and articulated that the boundaries between human animal and all other animals were severed. Not that they could not be crossed again and again in trance, as shamans all around the globe still do, but that the daily waking state of human consciousness was then separate from animal, changed, evolved. It was capable of extending itself along greater consciousness frequencies, capable of participating in the sentient web of consciousness that spreads across this universe.

At that time many, in what you might call bodhisattva-like devotion, saw the changes that future human beings would be going through. They chose to stabilize themselves in planetary consciousness, as sign posts, psychic "markers" in that vast and fluid changing realm. An older set of beings had made the same choice at the beginning of the Ice Age, when humans were sentient and yet still animal. Their spirits served to carry the fragile human community through that time of icy challenge. As that era came to an end, we took their places as markers, and they continued their evolution beyond Earth connection.

We, the Earth Ancestors, locked ourselves into place in human consciousness out of our deep abiding love of what it means to be a human being. We are ancient. Our wisdom predates all religions on your world today, although what we taught your physical ancestors remains in the heart of all your faiths. We can step in and out of linear time, although that is not the only time there is. And as your history carries you to the end of this current era and the beginning of the next one, we who have been with you since its beginning make ourselves known to you again.

In the past, people turned directly to us for advice. But as information was codified, in story, song, memorized or written down, the connections between incarnate and discarnate humans were largely forgotten. Not lost, but obscured. Not discarded, but misunderstood. People forgot how to make those connections, except through trance or mind-altering substances or accident induced by trauma.

People at the end of the Ice Age could all talk to us as easily as you now talk to someone on a phone. Then in a period of less than two thousand years, as the ice withdrew and humans turned their attention to other matters, the close, intimate, constant connections between all incarnate and discarnate human beings changed. We did not go away, the Earth Ancestors. But you only opened up to us in trance, in vision, in dream. We sustained unconscious connections as you learned to live in the world in a different way. Till you came to the point in your history when you could both live in a world of technology *and* communicate with the discarnates. You needed to do this, in order to evolve in consciousness. But now it is time to own your skills and function out of a new wholeness.

What began with a planetary threat of death by ice now ends with your threat of death to the planet itself. But you survived the ice. You can survive your own inventions if enough of you are able to reconnect to the love in yourselves and begin to share it in the world.

There are many, many thousands of us here, Earth Ancestors. Some of us are connected to places on the planet itself, while others are bound to activities, actions, crafts, to groups of people. We are guides and teachers, pattern-carriers. We are woven into human consciousness. Many of us are the particular guides of the gay tribe, sharing our ancient wisdom with you, for we are planetary archivists. But above all—we are Friends.

As you evolve, we evolve also. As this next cycle of human history begins, we shall move on and some of you shall take our places, woven into human consciousness, as sign posts for the next cycle of incarnational history. You shall become the guardians of love and work and exploration. You shall join the flow of human sentient Earth energy, as it takes its rightful place in the universal web of consciousness, linking planet to planet, incarnate and discarnate, physical and non-physical. Joyfully. For the soul.

There are thousands and thousands of us, discarnate Earth Ancestors. We are with you all the time. All that is needed for us to reconnect is your turning toward us in stillness and speaking, your turning toward us in dream and allowing us to come through. Anyone can talk with us. Once, all human beings did it, and one day soon all human beings may be doing it again. For some, it will be easiest to begin by reaching out to someone you have known and loved who has left the physical realm. Talk to them, call on them. Feel their presence, remembering that not everyone will communicate in words. Some will see pictures, some will feel energy, others will simply move from a place of inspiration. Some will sense light, others will be filled with sound or with vibration. All of this is connection. Not words alone, but feeling, love.

Turn to us. We are waiting. Trust that the doors between incarnate and discarnate can be opened again. Move through that door from a place of love and wisdom in yourself, and expanded love and wisdom will meet you. Some will see us, some will hear our names. Many will find it easiest to sit quietly with paper and ask for words to be given through you. It may take time to tell the difference between what you write and what is written through you.

But we are all one, and it doesn't matter who said what you write, if it is loving, practical, spiritual and useful. We are all one, all connected. Let love come through, and it will guide you.

Call on us in love. Call on us when you sit alone and in your tribal circles. Call on the scouting ancestors of the East, the flute playing ancestors of the South, your shaman ancestors from the West, and your hunter ancestors from the North. Ancestors, grandfathers of the gay people, call on us in your meditations, and we will be with you to inspire, heal and guide you.

Searching for Gay History

In searching for gay history one must turn inward to the depths of self, or turn outward to those who carry the memories. It is not enough to go back to ancient Greece, or to samurai Japan, or to look at the cross-dressing shaman/healers in the tribal nations of the world. Because the fullness of gay history lies beyond what you call history.

At the end of the Ice Ages, human beings as a whole made fundamental consciousness choices that affect your lives to this day. Territory and property were invented as concepts by a people used to cold and scarcity on the material plane. A separation between power and nurturance was made by men and women, in an effort to understand themselves better. All of human history, and gay history, has been colored by those choices.

Gayness is a matter of vibration. Gay men are "tuned" differently than other men. This difference in vibration is what allows men who are drawn to men to recognize each other. They sound different than men who are tuned toward women. At the end of the time of ice, this tuning was still understood by everyone as a part of the fullness of human nature. A sensitive mother could often tell before her child was born that he had chosen to incarnate as a man tuned to men. She could feel the sound of his tuning in her body. A less sensitive mother might not be able to tell that, but the others around her would. And even if there were no others around, by the time that child was weaned, the mother always knew that this child was running a different energy than a boy who would be tuned to women. Fathers of boys knew this too, they knew that this tuning called forth different qualities in their sons. They had no fear of this gay tuning, not disgust or shame. All children were loved for who they had chosen to be as they came into the world. All children were loved for the necessity of their being in the world and for the world, exactly as they had chosen.

Parents still sense this in their sons, this tuning. But several thousand years of history have turned their responses from love to rejection. Unconsciously, in their wombs, mothers with gay sons may turn against them. Later, their rejection of those sons may create such guilt in them that they try to make up for it by clinging, by trying to lovingly switch their tuning. Fathers of gay sons may also reject them early on. They sense the tuning, but remain distant because there is no expectation of their being nurturant, so that boys who will grow up to love men lack the closeness of father they need, and carry their mother's sense of fault and guilt with them.

It was not this way in the Ice Age. It was not this way in the transitional period between the withdrawing of the ice and the start of what you now call history and the birth of civilization. In that time, this matter of tuning was still understood. Parents understood it and honored it. The tuning in a boy was seen as a doorway to skills needed by the people. Art, dance, music, healing, were seen as special gifts that could come with this tuning. And every family felt blessed that had such a person in it. It was an honor to that family, a useful connection.

Most children feel at some point in their childhood that their parents are not their real parents. Gay sons may feel this more often than others, for lurking in their unconscious minds may be the memory of a time when their biological parents gave them over to be raised by men who loved men, who lived together in small communities near the larger villages and towns they were born in. There were such communities of women too. Others will speak of them and remember them.

Parents of gay sons loved them, cherished them, and knew that at some point within a year or two of their weaning, it would be time for them to be given to others to finish raising them. Often, these other fathers had been visiting them since birth, and were uncles, cousins, friends. Boys were not handed over to strangers most of the time, except in isolated places where the communities of gay men were more widely scattered. But even there, word would go out amongst the people that a boy was born in such and such encampment who was tuned toward men. And eventually that message made it to the gay collective.

For gay men today, the time of coming out is a major rite of passage. It may happen at puberty, or later. But in the past, the rite of passage that set aside gay boys from the community they were born in came early. It was not connected to the blossoming of their sexual desire. It was tied to a realization of their tuning, their vibration, as boys who would grow into men who would, amongst other things, love men.

This was not a time when boys were given away, thrust out of the homes they knew and loved. They were told about this time and looked forward to it. It was a day of feasting for an entire family, for an entire village, when a young boy was given to the men who would father him. They came to the village of his birth with herbs and other gifts. Everyone knew that the boy that went with them would always return to them as friend, as apprentice healer, musician, midwife as they began their journey of disconnection from their bodies. Everyone wanted such a companion on the way, and rejoiced in the going off of one who would learn those skills, and come back to share them.

Gayness was not just about sex. It was seen as a vibration that called forth in someone certain needed skills, needed gifts. The two men who fathered him taught him what they themselves had been taught, creating a loving chain of wisdom that existed for generations and generations in human history, the forgotten history. And in silent ways, this chain lives on. It lives on in theatre, in dance, in music. It lives on in sex and loving. But it has lost its spiritual connection, its purpose. For gayness is far more than sex. And as men remember this who are tuned to other men, wisdom will begin to rise into consciousness that is ancient and healing and needed by all of humanity. None of this is recorded in history. It was forgotten by the time the myths of ancient Greece were being told. But the memory of it abides in the collective unconscious of all humanity. And it resides in the unconscious minds of all men who are tuned to other men.

It will be a healing for all gay men to deepen in meditation and remember these things, feel them in the body, see them in the mind. It will be a healing for all gay men to allow their bodies to experience the feeling in those villages, the sense of deep and vital belonging, of life purpose. For much of what kills now is a deep sense of not belonging, of having no real purpose in being here. So let this healing rise up in you. Sit quietly and open the mind to remembering. Remember a time when men who loved men lived together in loving communities. Remember a time when men who loved men joined together in pairs, to teach the young boys who came to them as sons. Remember the time when a life partner, a work partner, a heart's true companion, was freely chosen and joyfully cherished by all, by family and community. Remember that kind of a life and rejoice in it. It is a part of your history to be reclaimed. Ancient, but ever present in the less than conscious mind.

The world is not the same as it was then. This remembering is not about going back, but about reconnecting. About connecting to one's history in order to move ahead. The world is not the same as it was at the end of the Ice Age. Families are not the same. There may never be the kinds of villages the world saw then, as there will probably not be hunting parties and campfires and vision quests in the depths of dark, deep caves. We do not recall to you these villages in order to have you recreate them. We recall them to you to remind you of what is possible. At the end of the Ice Age, people lived in tribes. But as you sentient human beings prepare yourselves to take your place in the web of sentience that connects the galaxy, all of Earth becomes a single tribe, a single village. And how you live in that global village will not be the same as the way your ancestors lived. You may not have actual gay tribes. But you will create safe, healing, and nurturing places to gather in, for ceremonies, conversation, quiet, shelter, haven, connection to others like yourselves. There, the attributes of functioning on this frequency will be taught and shared, the spiritual attributes of what you call gayness, the heart-love that connects all men who are tuned to other men through time.

In scattered places on this planet, some of these villages actually did survive into what you call recorded history. In Bali and New Guinea there were villages, in Western Australia, Peru, and central China. They are not recorded in history, but they were there. There and in other places, struggling to sustain an ancient memory of purpose, of necessity, of function in the round of human existence. Some of the fairy lore of western Europe preserve a memory of these villages, in the stories of *fairies* "kidnapping" children.

When purposeful, spiritual connection is forgotten, the depth of sexual connection often takes its place. Sex points one in the right direction, deep into the self, into mystery. But sex alone is not the answer to the gay dilemma of the present, the sense of meaninglessness. A sense of spiritual participation in the community of the planet is the answer. For no one else will tell us of our purpose. Its discovery must come from ourselves. Men subtlely tuned to men carry the answer. It is our work to reclaim it, together.

Bonds between friends, sacred bonds between mates, bonds between incarnate and discarnate. Let us rejoice in all of them. When joy flows out from us, the world will know us as we are and cease to fear. Disease will be transmuted. Of this there is no doubt.

Other Gay Realities

What you call gay is a pattern of vibrations, a certain weaving together of vibrations. It does not exist only in the physical realm. It exists in other realms also. And just as there are gay guides and gay angels, there are gay heavens, and planets where gayness is integrated into the fabric of sentient life in ways that you on Earth have both forgotten and are moving toward again.

Picture in your minds a perfect, cloudless sky, a sky of turquoise blue. Turquoise, not Earth blue. And feel the warmth of a sun that is larger than the sun you know, but silver-white in color, not yellow-golden. There are trees in this place. Forests. But many of them are red, or indigo. This is a world, a kind of a world. It is a dream world, a paradise as many people have dreamed of one. But this paradise is yours, a gay one. It is called Thelki. Feel this place, allow yourself to wander its paths and its mountains. There is food abundant, warmth, nothing to fear, only love. Its nights are mild, with a sky filled with unfamiliar constellations, with many, many small topaz moons circling above. And the people of this world are ancient, wise, strong, and gay, as you are. They are god-like, goddess-like. Men and women both, mythic, splendid, real as all gods and heroes are real.

Sometimes, two human beings have the same dream. It is ephemeral, gone when they awake from it. But Thelki is a dream place, created by discarnate human beings, so solidly of subtle energy as to be enduring. It is older than time, and constantly being re-created. It is the focus of discarnate energy, and a source of connection and healing for incarnate gay folk. Thelki is real, it is the heaven gay people yearn for. It is a spring to drink from, a land of endless rivers. Thelki means, "Liquid place that is infinitely, fluidly changing." Water-wet, constantly changing, Thelki is a place that you can walk through when you need a healing of the soul. You do not have to die to go there. All that you have to do is close your eyes, see the sparkling turquoise of its sky, feel yourself walking beside a clear, rushing stream. Breathe in the warmth of a silver sun, breathe in the purity of its air. That is Thelki. And if for even an instant you had a sense of it, then you were there and can go back again. To Thelki, the land that refreshes. To Thelki, the land of gay energy.

Thelki is real and not real, as a powerful dream is. Its rivers and mountains and people are real and not real. They are real as the gods of your planet are real. There are gay gods and heroes in Thelki, like Reydehn, Enthras, Kuniata, and Relag. In knowing about Thelki, you can go there yourself—now. And it is now that concerns us. For to step into the turquoise-living NOW of Thelki is to make a healing in yourself that will ripple out to all gay people, and therefore, to the whole of your world. For love is the only healing. And what runs endlessly liquid, wet and changing through the heart of Thelki is love. Love knows no gender, love is neither male nor female. Love is an energy that permeates the universe. It is eternal, infinite, and capable of flowing everywhere. Love can fill the hearts of all living beings, in physical bodies and out of them. So turn to Thelki now, and turn to love. To a place of love, a realm of love, a source of love flowing endlessly.

Everything physical concerns patterns of vibration. Different physical objects can exist in the same place at the same time—if they are vibrating at different frequencies. So there are several different planet Earths, co-existing in the same space/time location, at different frequencies. Some of these Earths have no life on them at all. Some have no human life. There is one parallel Earth in which the human beings are of one gender only. There is an Earth in which human sexuality and reproduction have not diverged from earlier animal habits. But there is also one parallel Earth in which gayness is a fully accepted and functional part of human life there. It is just as common for a world leader, female, to have a female spouse as a male one, just as common for a leading entertainer, male, to have a male spouse as a female one. On that Earth, fear and divisiveness have not taken root the way they have on the Earth that you are incarnate on.

There was a time when the "doorways" between the different Earths were more fully open. There was more interweaving between Earths from one life to another. And there was more telepathic connection between them in the past also. But now it is time to knock on those doors again. Now is the time to sit in meditation and reach out. One of the many Earths may destroy itself via nuclear disaster. But that can be averted on *all* Earths by communicating peace from Earth to Earth to Earth.

For gay people, it is useful to reach out to the Earth where gayness is a part of life. It will give you integrated role models, give you emotional support, give you inspiration. To reach a non-physical reality like Thelki is spiritually nurturing, but to know another physical world, with physical inhabitants incarnate in bodies just like yours, will be strengthening and useful. One of the fundamental historical differences between that world and yours is that Alexander the Great did not die in the east, but lived to extend his empire to the west, across both sides of the Mediterranean to the Atlantic. He ruled it with his beloved friend Hephestion. There, the hints of gayness you ascribe to your Jesus were manifest. There David loved Jonathan proudly, and did not have to meet him secretly in a field. To some an Earth such as this is a fiction. But fiction or fact, you can tap into it and feel the joy of men's love for each other reach out and fill you with its beauty.

Before a sentient species incarnates, it will create Practice Realities where it can test out patterns of culture on a subtle plane. What you call Lemuria and Atlantis were practice runs established before complete incarnation. You know of these two, with their achievements and failures, but it has only been recently that you have been ready to open up to the memories of a third civilization, one that was so eminently successful that your species knew it was ready for complete incarnation. This civilization occupied a "lost continent" in the Indian Ocean called Kandayata. This continent was mountainous, with many rivers. Its people were blue of skin, and memory of them and their glorious civilization filtered into India, Tibet, Arabia and Africa. The Garden of Eden was in Kandayata. The Tree of Life grew on the sacred mountain of Kandayata. And in Kandayata the love between men was understood and valued, as was the love between women, and the love between women and men. It is time for all of humanity to remember a "lost civilization" where love in all its forms was honored as sacred. It is time for all of humanity to remember the test run, the "blue print" reality—where everything was holy, where there was no separation between form and spirit, where everyone got it right. This balance was present in the very first civilization on your world, in Ushtu in Africa, which flourished before the Ice Ages began. Let memories of Ushtu awaken in your minds also, Ushtu the mother of all Earth cultures.

There are many realities that resonate with the gay energy. In your meditations, work to find them. There are gay worlds, gay guides, gay angels. In the Pleiades, your Milky Way's sibling galaxy, there are numerous planets with integrated gay life. So too in other parts of your galaxy. Be adventurous in your meditations. Roam the galaxy, roam the heavens. You are not alone. You are not alone. You are not alone.

AIDS and the Healing Process

A disease can only take hold in a physical body when there are prior imbalances in the mind and in the subtle bodies. It is not hard to understand how mental imbalances can occur in "marginal" peoples such as gay men, drug users, Africans. But from that base, this disease spreads out to anyone with subtle body imbalances.

The primary imbalance has been mentioned already. AIDS appears in people who believe that they do not belong here. Anyone born here is a native of this planet, and belongs here as much as everyone else. To those who still carry the sense of not belonging, we suggest the following exercise.

Sit in a chair with your feet on the floor. Close your eyes, become aware of your heartbeat and the in-and-out flow of your breath. Now begin to feel that there is a soft amber light, warm and healing, rising up from the ground, and entering your feet. If you cannot sit up, visualize this energy entering your feet from whatever position you are in. Feel this amber light fill your feet, your legs. Your trunk, arms, head. This light is Earth-light. It is healing, grounding, and will help to reconnect you to the part of you that belongs here, was born here, was born here for a reason, in spite of what you or others may tell you. Feel this light move into every part of your body, every muscle, organ, bone, every cell. Feel yourself glowing with it. Feel it pouring out the tips of your fingers and the top of your head. Feel this light entering the wounded, disconnected places in your mind. Feel it weave you into earthness, healing you and cleansing you.

Gender imbalance in an individual on a subtle body level can also be a clue to the weakenings that may invite AIDS to manifest. There must be an inner balance between female and male, between strength and nurturing. Societal roles do not encourage this balance, especially for gay men. For generations, gayness in men was seen as a factor of excess femaleness. In reaction to that, some contemporary gay men have rejected the female and gone the other way. Often, the female rises up in a gay man, but he rejects it in fear of losing the gayness he has worked so hard to claim. Do you feel balanced in both genders? Here is a meditation you can use to help you balance them.

Close your eyes and feel your body. Touch it softly with your hands. Feel its manness, its shape, size, tone. Smile as you touch yourself, and take pleasure in being a man, in being the man that you are, as you are. No two trees are the same, no two men are the same. Feel that you are alive and beautiful as you are, unique and a part of the world. When that feeling is strong in you, imagine that someone has superimposed a second body into the space where you are. This body is female. It is the woman you would have been if you had entered this current life as a girl. Feel the energy of that body, the experiences in that body. Know that that alternate you is a part of you, an inner, real part of who you are. Let your consciousness drift back and forth between the male and female you. What feelings are similar in each? Which are different? New? Can you own both and move back and forth joyfully and easily? Keep doing this until you can.

All of us have a dark side, a shadow. It includes all of the traits we do not like about ourselves. This shadow exists on the subtle energy plane. All our fear, anger, pain may be there, trapped, hidden, while we pretend on the outside to be happy, healthy, fine. Practice conjuring up this dark second self. Feel it rise up behind you. Get to know it, get to know the power that resides in it, that we deny until we reclaim it. Slowly, let this shadow of you enter your body. All kinds of emotions may rise up, so you may want to do this with someone else, with someone around you can talk about this with. At first, the shadow may not even want to enter your body, and you may be revolted by it. But in time, as the two of you get to know each other, you will be able to sit, stand, lie in the same place. When you become one, the energy you used to hold those parts of you at bay will be freed for other purposes. And you will not have to fear the rising up of the shadow. As it becomes conscious, you will also be able to reason with it, control it, transmute its nature by understanding why you buried it in the first place.

There is a second shadow, another aspect of the self. This aspect is seldom talked about. We call it the golden shadow. It is hidden like the other shadow, but what is repressed is not negative, but positive. The golden shadow contains all those wonderful, healing, transformative qualities that we have denied in ourselves, often because they would set us apart, call attention to ourselves, or simply because they are qualities our society does not acknowledge, psychic and healing skills for example. Now, feel your golden shadow. Feel a golden presence gathering around you. Invite it in, invite it into your body and your conscious self. Feel its wisdom, feel its gifts. Know that they are yours, are a part of you. Own them, become whole with them. In the golden shadow is the wisdom to understand why we invited AIDS into our lives, and how we can heal ourselves of it. Will this healing be through continuing in the same body, or through leaving it? This we decide for ourselves, and the golden light that fills us can help us to make that choice consciously.

These exercises seem simple, but they can help you to make a change in your subtle bodies that will ripple into the physical. You may not sense the subtle aspects of yourself, so isn't a simple exercise appropriate, a subtle one? Know that you are female and male, shadow and light, know that you are a part of this world and belong here.

The thymus gland in the body is directly concerned with the healing process. This gland often atrophies as one grows older. You can send energy to your thymus to strengthen it, you can visualize it growing and functioning well. Feel the area of your body just above the ribs, midway between the throat and the heart. This is the thymus region. Feel an aqua or turquiose blue light glowing there, feel it spreading out from there until it fills your entire body. As you do this, say to yourself or out loud "I am a spiritual warrior. I am invincible." The thymus is the seat of spiritual warrior strength. The power of the spiritual warrior is not war, but peace. When you do this exercise, you generate peace in your body. Then, whether you choose to live in the body or out of it, you will live as an invincible warrior, and make the healing that is appropriate to you in this moment.

Much of what creates the foundation of any illness is the feeling of being alone. Infants die who are not held and touched. Without intimacy, the immune system suffers and turns on itself. Men suffer greatly from lack of intimacy. No wonder we die sooner than women. Part of our sense of self is connected to work. But to satisfy that need leaves little energy for closeness. And it does not help that men are continually told we do not know how to relate, cannot relate. And it is worse when two men come together who have been told this. The following exercise is designed to help you make a healing in this place.

Close your eyes, and keep your inner eyes closed too. This is a meditation about feelings. Do not picture the perfect lover, what he looks like, or what kinds of things you will do together. Close your eyes and let yourself *feel* what it will be like to be with a man who you love and who loves you in return. Move into your heart and feel the warmth that gathers there. Let yourself feel the love that flows between your bodies. Feel the tenderness, the closeness.

Feel what it is like to be held through the night by someone you love, as you hold him. Let joy sing out from your body. Feel your love ripple out into the world. Feel it touch others and fill them with love too. Let your love be like a beacon. Let your love be a song. Touch your body in all its sad and lonely places and say to it that this is what it will feel like to be loved. And know that as you do this you heal the inner place that says you can't be loved, can't love. Now embrace this inner lover, hold him, become him, and know that he is you.

The inner child carries wounds that can fester and invite disease. You cannot heal the body of the man who doesn't feel love without healing the boy in you too, who grew up hating himself for being different. Who hated himself for his capacity to love, and turned away from that part of himself.

Go back in time. Find the places, the different ages, when the boy you were was wounded. Some people have to go back before birth. Some people have different ages to be healed, others have one. Go back. Find that boy. Face him. Hold him. Take him in your lap and hug him and tell him that everything will be all right. Only one thing wounds, really—not being loved as we are. So go back and love yourself as you were, as no one loved you then. Hold your boy self and rock him and heal him. Tell him that this pain he feels will end, that he will grow and change and stop being a victim of other people's fear and unlovingness. Do this again and again till he can smile and laugh and rejoice with you. For the wounds that are healed in the body of the boy will generate greater healing in the man that boy has become. And when he has learned to love this part of himself, he can be loved as he is, he can love others.

We know about viruses and T-cells. We also need to know about inner healing. AIDS begins with inner imbalances.

The viral factors are the middle of the story. These little exercises are by no means the whole of the story of inner healing. Many are doing this work now. Many are remembering our ancient-future healing gifts. And there are many ways to do this work. This is but a single one of them. Also know and feel the love of the discarnate ones who give these tools. Feel our presences and our love surrounding you. You are not alone. None of us is alone. All sentient life is connected, in physical bodies and out of them.

Daily life leaves its mark upon one, in the physical and the subtle bodies. Some of what we carry is a gift, and some of what we carry is a burden that weakens the immune system. Part of the healing process is to release the "negative" energy we carry. Fear, sorrow, pain, self-hatred, judgements about our own and others' worth, the criticism of our parents, the anger of siblings, the shaming of teachers and friends, all of that can be released.

Imagine a sphere of golden light around you. Feel it spinning around your body. As it spins it has the power to draw out, transmute, release whatever energy exists in your body that is unwanted. Move through your life, and focus on the negativity inside. If you find anything that you do not want to carry, feel it being drawn out of your body and into the spinning sphere, like iron filings drawn up to a magnet. Feel the release and the cleansing. Feel yourself grow lighter each time you let go. Whatever blocks or clogs your own pure energy can be released. Into the light. Out of your body. This letting go and completing can be difficult. Sometimes we would rather hold onto pain than have nothing at all. But this process of letting go will make room in you for new ties, for clearer energy. When you are willing to unclog yourself, your healing will advance as you desire on the deepest levels. To live or to die, you might as well clean house. Release those who are still tied to you, whose wounds you carry, and remember that no one hurts another who has not been wounded oneself. But you do not need to keep hurting yourself by carrying old pain. Release it to the golden sphere. Allow the golden light to fill the emptied places. As the sun warms and blesses, use this light to heal and bless.

We Are Midwives for the Dying

Life does not begin at birth or end at death. Life extends beyond body and time, into and out of a spaciousness like the most powerful of dreams. Words alone cannot describe it. Perhaps 3-D film might one day do it, reveal the fluid vastness that life is. But one aspect of life is creating a body to focus yourself in. To do this is holy, to do this is a gift. You live in many bodies, as a painter paints many canvasses. Death is not the destruction of the artist. Death is the beginning of another phase in your timeless creativity.

Gayness is the coming together of certain strands of humanness. This particular arrangement, particular frequency, resonates well with certain functions in the human community. It is a nurturing frequency, a strong and caring one, that expresses itself in every possible way, yet excels at certain ones. To make art, to dance, to make beauty of body, food, home, all of these can be gifts of this energy. But working with those who are dying, working with death, is one of the skills that have been forgotten, not only by your community, but by the world itself. And many have died without the comforting hand of son, cousin, friend. But time brings all powers back to themselves. Time makes you remember this.

How do you work with death? How do you work with fear and rage and pain? Only love can help you do this. Only turning inward again and again to find the flicker of your inner love can nurture you enough to be powerful enough to work with death. Once you turn inward you can draw out a strand of love and offer it to someone who is dying. But it isn't your love that they take. Your love is a thing they taste. And having tasted it, say to them, "This love is a drop of water in the sea of love it comes from. And death is the invitation to swim freely in that sea again."

Touch is a healing. Do not be afraid of it. Sit quietly and draw energy into the bottoms of your feet from the core of the Earth. Let it fill your entire body until it is pouring out the ends of your fingers and out the top of your head. Then draw the energy of the heavens down into the top of your head. Let it fill your body until it pours out your hands and your feet. Then—only then—you can touch someone and bring them healing. Then, and only then can you touch someone without using up your own energy. You are charged by Earth and heaven. You use their energy to heal. This prevents burn out of your circuits. Keep doing this to recharge yourself. And teach it to your dying friends.

Some people will not want to hear that life does not begin at birth or end at death. For many gay people, the sense of spirituality has been for so long denied that only the body, sex, beauty seems real. And it will be hard for some gay men to hear that there is more than that, that rises up from spirit and goes back to it again. But you can say these things silently, and the unconscious part of the person dying will hear you nonetheless. You can silently beam love out from your heart to the heart of your dying friend, and it will get there. You can beam words out of your third eye to theirs, and they will hear it. Nothing is wasted in friendship, nothing is wasted in experience. All words will be heard and remembered. Your caring thoughts will reach their destination.

Some who are dying will find doors in consciousness opening. Some rejoice in that, some are frightened by it. Your being there to talk about the spiritual, about the presence of "unseen" guides and friends, friends who have died already, who are waiting to welcome them beyond death will be useful. Often those dying will be visited in visions and dreams by loved ones who have died. To some this is a joy, to others this sign of death approaching is a seal upon their sense of failure in their body-life. Comfort them. Hold them. Let them know that no life is wasted, that it is time to forgive themselves the seeming failures, time to rejoice in simply having lived, eaten, laughed, smelled a flower, even suffered. All that happens to us is what we draw to us to learn from. And remind them that they are not done, but in a certain sense, just beginning. Beginning another joyful phase in the aspects of their life that your culture prevents you from knowing. For life in and out of bodies is woven together, the seed of one eternal in the fullness of the other. Not one a place of grace, the other a fall, but each woven together in sacredness. Each floating in a vaster state of Oneness.

There are tools that you can use in your work, you gay men who have chosen to be midwives for the dying. We offer you several now, to add to your work, to experiment with. Drugs are tools, different kinds of treatments and therapies are tools. The information that we offer is a tool. But it is important to remember that a tool is something to assist one in one's work. When a tool does not work, there is a tendency to get angry at the tool, to blame the tool for not facilitating the healing. But sometimes, the wrong tool is used in a job. And in the case of dying, you cannot make a person heal or die well if they do not want to. And if they do, your tool does not do the work, and you do not do the work, you are only there to help them do it for themselves.

After a child is born, the midwife cuts the umbilical cord. When someone is dying, it is important to try and cut the binding cords before someone dies. One of the jobs of a midwife to the dying is to help them do that. Help them move into a meditative state where they can feel the unfinished business that binds them to others. They need not deal with those people directly, nor may they be able to. But to send love to all those people, to forgive and to ask for forgiveness, will loosen those ties that make it more difficult to disconnect from the body. Help them to see those ties as fibers connecting them, and help them to see how this process unravels those fibers and releases them.

Sound can be used in this process. It can soothe and settle the physical body. It can lessen pain. But most important of all it is effective at changing the vibratory pattern in the physical body and the subtle body so that when the time comes for the subtle form to withdraw from the physical, there is no fear in the body or the mind. The best sound to be used for this is the deepest "Oh" sound you can make. It should come from the bottom of your throat, and it should make your ribs vibrate. It's a long O, as in "know." Which you can help someone to make himself. Or if you are in a situation where you cannot make the sound out loud, to even whisper it, or just to feel its vibration and direct it through your hands or your mind to the person dying will bring them comfort.

If they are too weak to make sound, you can help those in pain, those dying, by showing them how to feel the movement of breath in their abdomen. Often the fear of losing breath is a constriction in the chest that comes from shallow breathing. Moving down into the abdomen and feeling the rise and fall from there brings a deeper breath in, expands the lung's capacity.

The visual pattern to the right may help to alleviate pain, and ease the process of unraveling the subtle from the physical. The eyes will wander, but if one keeps bringing them back to the dot at the center, it will stimulate an altered state of consciousness in the person looking at it. If someone can copy it in their own hand, however roughly, that is good, but they need not do that to have this visual pattern be effective.

There are two additional visual patterns that you can make use of in your journey. Copy them both in your own hand if possible.

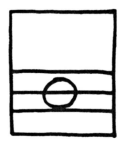

Use this pattern to support you when you want to be present in your physical body, during the process of unraveling, for those times when you need to function in your physical body. Stare at it, try to see it imprinted inside yourself. It will help to connect your physical and non-physical bodies.

When you know that you are ready to un-

ravel the subtle connections between spirit and matter, use the pattern to the left to support you in releasing, in traveling, in moving on beyond the physical. Visualize this pattern outside of your body, and see it also inside, slowly moving up from root to heart to crown. It will help to untie the strands between physical and non-physical.

You as soul create many bodies to express yourself through, in different times, in different places, as female and male, as straight and gay. You are born many times and you die many times. Death is that part of the soul's process of recreating itself. The work of gay midwives to the dying is not easy. But you can tap into the place where you have done it before. You can tap into your guides, you can tap into the source of love, which permeates the universe. Love binds all together. No one is separate from love, from spirit. And death is not a separation. It is only a change in frequency.

Redefining the Sacred

There was a time when what is called "the sacred" was well-defined. Certain places were sacred. Walls were built around them, incense burned, candles lit. And certain days were sacred. Not the day before or the day after. But this day, in a certain month, a special moon. And not everyone agreed as to what was sacred, but everyone's rules were about distinctions. This is profane. But that, that is—sacred. This action is sacred, if you do it this way. But that act is definitely not sacred, and never will be. You'll go directly to hell if you do that.

But the world is changing. Human consciousness is changing. And as life becomes increasingly more spiritually attuned, the barriers between sacred and not sacred are changing. Certain places are sacred, sometimes. Certain days are sacred, certain acts, if they feel that way. In place of rigid barriers, there are fluid ones. And this will become more common, that the sacred will rise up from an ordinary conversation, or a table will become an altar for a sacramental meal that was a desk an hour before, and may be the setting for a heated game of cards an hour later.

When things change, people often cling to the old rules. And it does little good to tell them that in exchange for seven very sacred days in each calendar year, and ten half holy days, there will now be the possibility of every single day being sacred, if they attune themselves to that energy. No good saying that the temple, shrine, church, mosque, may be converted into co-op apartments, but that every living room, bedroom, street, gym, bus terminal, has the capacity to become the center of the entire universe, for a while, if everyone in it perceives it that way. People like distinctions. It is going to take a while for would-be priestesses and priests to discover the fluid rules of their transmuted vocations.

Gay people have a function in this time of transition, a vital and necessary spiritual function. The weaving together of vibrations that is now called gayness is not the average pattern on your world. It is not average, but it is important. To be gay is to have a different relationship to male and female. To be gay is to have a different relationship to young and old. To be gay is to transcend other groups, political, social, ethnic, religious. And the experiences gained from all these differences are useful to the whole of the human community.

To be whole is to be balanced in one's male and female energies, whether straight or gay, but gay people are often more attuned to the non-manifest energy. To not have one's sexuality connected to reproduction creates a different sense of inner child in gay people. One does not expect to leave the child behind in order to be parent to their children.

Gay people are born into all families, in all races, countries, classes, religions. In the old days, the experiences of gay people were important in holding communication lines open. Men and women in relations with each other could find mediators in their gay kin, because of the different relation to gender gay folk have. Adults and children each found that gay relatives could relate to them and help them bridge the gap between them. Communities depended upon gay runners, message bearers, scouts, who would travel to other communities and connect with gay folk there. Gay people were often the peace makers, because of their fluidity.

When gay people are not honored in a society, and when they have forgotten their inherent skills, then the entire community suffers. Families lose their mediators, groups lack their connectors. It is time for gay folk to start remembering who they are, why they exist, what they can do in the world, for the world. There are generations of wounded gay people. Many are more out of touch with the other gender, inner and outer, more than straight people, who have the outer reflection to remind them of wholeness. And a people with no children have become trapped in their inner child places, spoiled, hurt, sulking. So in place of the communication between communities gay people ought to create, there is only silent furtive sex connecting them.

It is time for the gay community to heal itself. It is time for the gay community to assume the place in the human community that it was created for. It is time for men to come together in loving communities, to explore their inner femaleness so that they can help men and women communicate. It is time for gay men to own their capacity for youthfulness and their ability to be wise elders, so that they can once again sit with a child and be an adult who remembers being a child, so that they can talk to parents who thought they needed to forget their inner child in order to have children of their own. And it is time for gay people to start using for planetary transformation the global network that already exists, spreading information, love, advice, support, money, food, clothing.

The gay community can heal. It will not heal from focusing on combating disease alone. A healing must include a spiritual element. And that is what has often been withheld from gay people. The religious communities of this planet have for the most part excluded, or at best ignored, their gay members. But religion is not necessarily spirituality. And it is through a spiritual connection, not a religious one, that the human community of this planet will find its healing.

What is spiritual, what is sacred, is being redefined. It is being redefined in a fluid way. Gay people, by their very nature, exist in a state of internal fluidity that will make us vital in this time of planetary challenge. As we enter the age called Aquarius, it is useful to remember that the constellation Aquarius represents the youth Ganymede, who Zeus took up to Mount Olympus to be cupbearer to the gods, and his own lover. Gay people have a share in this coming transformation. To the ancient Egyptians, the water carrier was the source of the Nile, pictured as a man with breasts. When Jesus was preparing for his last Passover, it is recorded in Luke that he sent his disciples into the city to meet a man carrying a jar of water, in a culture where only women were supposed to carry water.

Let us carry the water of love again, the water of life. This is our role in the community of human beings. This is our share in the world's redefining of the sacred. When we remember our own sacredness, we help to heal the world. We bring together families. We bring together countries. We use our fluid natures to make change. We remember what is sacred in us, and we rejoice in it again.

Sacred Sex / Spiritual Love

Many of your religions reject physicality. They call it ugly, dark, a prison for the soul. They forget that each soul creates its own body. They forget that physicality can be so filled with joyful possibility that a soul would rather create a body in the slums of Calcutta than exist forever in the discarnate planes. There is pain and suffering in physicality, because it is easy to forget the challenges of life in a physical body. But to live in a body, to create a body and fill it with life—that is a sacred blessing of the soul. There is purpose and beauty and joy in physicality. It can take many lifetimes to understand this. But does two plus five stop being seven if a child doesn't understand it yet?

Physical life is a gift, a blessing, a divine opportunity for the soul to express itself, the soul's canvas. No one physical life can express, can contain, the fullness of the soul's abundant timelessness. Birth and death, rebirth and dying again allow the soul the opportunity to "try on lots of different clothes." Death is not a stealing away of the gift of life, a negation of it. Death allows the gift of life to be renewed when a certain "style" of beingness has "gone out of fashion" for you.

Physical life is a gift and a blessing. It allows you to shape and mold the experiences, the wisdom, the information you have gathered about existence into a solid, yet constantly changing form.

Physical life is a gift of blessing, and love that is physically expressed is one of the greatest joys of all possible existences. Discarnate, two lovers can "stand" in each other's bodies, merge together and vibrate in and out of each other. But there is nothing in the non-physical realms quite like the touch of a hand on skin, the wonderful slide of lips, the magnificent joy of two pressing against each other's limitations in order to express the inexpressible. Love can be sacred. The dance of making love can be an expression of spiritual delight more resonant than a chorus full of angels singing out at the top of their lungs. It can be the opportunity for two together to share from the depths the wisdom, the experience, the cosmic information that they have gathered in their dance through existence.

People have forgotten that spiritual love can be expressed through sacred sex. They have forgotten spirituality, they have forgotten what is truly sacred. What is sacred is that which attunes physical and subtle energies. A song can be sacred, a bowl of rice, a photograph of a dog and a child, a laugh, a sigh, a kiss. The potential for sacredness is ever-present, just as the possibility of love is ever-present—simply because you exist.

Love is a vibration that permeates the physical universe. Love is the vibration from which the physical universe emerged. Love is the nature of God, of Spirit. Sacred sex happens when two attune themselves to the Source of All. Sacred sex rises up from spiritual love. It rises up from it and carries you back to it. Two together, dancing across the altar of a bed enact the sacrament of this universe beginning. We call it sacred sex. Once all humans knew that sex should only happen if it is sacred. We call it spiritual love because people have forgotten that that is what true love is. We call it making love, for that is what it is, to make the energy of love ripple out into the world through the movements and feelings of your bodies.

Once, sacred spaces were built on power spots on the planet. They were aligned with the directions and served as energy-collecting points on days when earth, moon and sun were in certain powerful relations. Priesthoods served to channel those energies. But now, everything has the potential to be sacred. Your bed is a sacred space. The candle that you light may be holy. You are priests. The movements you make can fill the universe with subtle energy.

You love another man who is tuned to the same vibration. Your bodies sing around the same notes. You bring the song of life up in each other's bodies. Your bodies become trumpets, horns, flutes, singing out sacredness. And you cannot help but bring your music closer. You need to blend together your portions of the sacred hymn made flesh. The song of life in your bodies is the music of spiritual love made manifest. You are priests of the sacred, bio-electrical technicians wiring physical and subtle energies together. The song of life runs electric through your bodies. Hand touches hand, and the current builds, the song builds. Face to face, body to body. You wire yourselves together in sacred music.

The holy power of union connects you in your bodies and carries you beyond them at the same time. You do not leave the physical. The song of life expands as it courses through you. The rush of orgasm, the drumming, the chorus, the fire, the waterfall, joins worlds together for a moment, and carries priests into the holy of holies which is the seed-bed of the physical world itself. For some say that the only purpose of love-making is procreation. But we say this—that the purpose of making love is to carry two lovers back to that fluid, ever-present state of power from which the physical was born. When two together do this, go there, bring up that music in their bodies, it is holy. Whenever two go back there, the energy that birthed the world is released back into it, anew. To bless, cleanse, recharge. For spiritual love expressed in sex becomes a sacred experience that weaves these worlds together. It is the mystery of returning to the beginning of time, to the source of grace. Alone, only great saints can do this. They are rare. But through this doorway, any two can reach that birthing place, bathe in the springs of its sweetness, carry that blessing out with them into the world of form. Sex alone, desire, lust, cannot generate enough energy to move two lovers to this place. But when two hearts are echoing with love, then this journey to the sacred becomes the vehicle for transformation, transmutation. Traveling out of time. Traveling back to time's beginning. Spun through the portals of space. Spiraling through them. In order to fill the world with song.

How To Become A Virgin

Before you loved another man, your body had a power of newness to it. Your circuits were clear and pulsing with your own pure energy. One way to heal yourself, one way to make yourself open to the kind of heart-centered love that you are seeking, is to become a virgin again. For every man who has ever touched you has left his joy, his pain, his love, his sorrow with you.

To become a virgin again is to become whole in and of and with yourself. It is to stand poised again in all your beauty between Earth and Heaven. You will never be too old to do this, cannot be with too many others to bring yourself back to this place again.

This is a ritual to do for yourself, by a tub, a pool, a lake or by the ocean. Sit quietly. Deepen into yourself. Close your eyes and connect with your breath. Feel the Earth beneath your feet, and draw its energy up into your body with each inhalation. Draw it into your heart and hold it there. Now feel the energy of Heaven, and with each inhalation draw it down through the top of your head into your heart. Feel the twining of these two energies in your body. Feel them illuminating your heart.

Move backwards in time now, remembering every man and woman that you have ever shared sexual energy with. From the most recent, move slowly backward to the earliest of your sexual partners. If pain or anger or resentment or sorrow comes up for you when you think of a particular person, release that energy down into the earth when you exhale. Let the earth transmute that energy like dung, to fertilize and enrich itself. And if joy and love and bliss comes up for you when you think of a particular person, release that energy through the top of your head, give it back to the heavens to make new stars.

Each time that you exhale, you will become lighter and lighter. Each time that you exhale, not only will you become freer, but you will be serving to release those people whose energy you still carry in your body. You may not remember individuals, but rooms, places, times in your life. Release them. Breathe out and as you do this, thank all these people and places for having shared their beingness with you. The information you have exchanged with them will remain. But the strands that connect you to them will be cut away. You will be free and they will be free. And eventually you will bring yourself back to the place and time in your life when you were a virgin, when no one else's energy circulated through the fibers of your energy body except your own.

Go back to the young man you were then. Go back to the young man you were that still lives within you. Go back to the young man you were, who had not opened or been opened to another person yet in a sexual way. Close your eyes and feel how he felt, how he moved, how he ate and slept and dreamed. Go back to the power that young man had, of youth and newness and life untouched. Breathe that power into your body, breathe that power into all the cells of your body. Release his fear and pain and loneliness back down into the earth. Release his boyhood dreams and fantasies out to the stars. Breathe in the purity of his aloneness. Be married to yourself now. Be fully empowered—and one with yourself.

Alone now, cleansed now, step into the water. Be it tub, pool, lake, or ocean, step into the water and let it embrace you. Be with the water and be with your breath. Cup your hands, scoop up that water, raise it up to the heavens and baptise yourself with it. Pour it down over your head. Pour it over your heart, your genitals, your ass, over every part of your body. Now you are cleansed. Now you are whole. Now you are a virgin again. Step out of the water. Step out of the water whole and cleansed. Step out into the world in all your power. Step out into the world with pure and open heart—to love for the first time again. As a virgin, a strong virgin, a wise virgin. As the man you always knew you were.

A Ritual for Two Men

Make a holy space. Define it by crystals or candles, or whatever you two choose to make a boundary with.

Outside your holy circle is the world of time and space. Within it is the world of spirit.

To make this circle is to shift your consciousness. You sit in the circle face to face and gaze deeply into each other's eyes. You breathe and move with breath. You drift into a state of consciousness expanded beyond that which is familiar in your day-to-day life.

You face one another, naked. All the beauty of the other fills your eyes. You are blessed by the heart of each other's spirit. True beauty. Love beauty. Radiant.

Feel the energy between you begin to turn. Feel it circle and expand. Feel it rising up between you in the center of the circle, in a great column of light. Feel it rise up into the heavens. Feel it spin deep down into the earth.

Your bodies glow with love. Your love creates the column of light in the space between your bodies.

Whisper, "Peace, peace, peace." Whisper, "Holy, holy, holy." Whisper, "Love, love, love." See and feel and hear and rejoice in all the senses of planetary transformation that wash through you. Joy. Communication. Comfort for all. The end of war. The end of AIDS. Send these dream feelings, wish feelings, future memory senses out into the column of light. Know that they are broadcast to the heavens and to the living Earth itself. Let all the world know, let the universe know, that two human male lovers come together in a sacred way, to work the work of healing for this world.

Love is. Love transforms. With one hand, touch each other, gently. Touch, lovers. Feel the sparkling electric radiance of each other's beingness. Moving deep into each other's eyes, weaving them together, use your other hand to move toward orgasm. Slowly. Pacing each other if you can. Touching self and touching the other. Whispering "peace, love, holy." Whispering "love, holy, peace." Whispering your visions of joy and freedom and healing and transformation in this world.

And when the moment approaches, when the moment comes that your body is about to release the deep seed of itself, intensify your planetary vision, as breath rises, quickens. Feel the energy rise up in your body, feel the energy of orgasm be released into the central column of light. The light of your bodies intensifies its light. Heaven and Earth know your love, feel it, share it. For the energy of your love is beamed out, beamed down. Holy. Electric. Sacred. Your thoughts are energy. You turn them into light. This light connects you, fills the circle, and expands beyond it in a column of your healing visions, out into the world. The column of light now fills the circle. It is timeless, it is endless, it is sacred. You have touched the beginning of time and gone beyond it. You have touched the primal darkness and emerged from it—as light.

When breath slows, when heart stops pounding, as light travels out beyond you and then fades, feel the light that is still present in your bodies. Feel the love you share that generated the light. And touch each other, hold each other close. Breathe deeply once together, and exhale strongly. This will close your circle. Gather up stones, blow out candles. Let the sacred weave itself into space and time, gay priests.

The Body Is a Doorway to Wisdom

Love is information exchange between individuals. Information is the division of Absolute Consciousness into absorbable units. Information can be exchanged through the mind, the body, the subtle body. The question to ask when moving toward someone, when thinking of friendship, when contemplating sexual connection, is, "Do I want to hold the information this person has absorbed in my system?" Information flows easily. But it is easier to take it in than to release it. Easier to give than to un-give.

Deep love is profound sustained information exchange. Lovers find beauty in each other's information. They find beauty in the ways they use it, to live in the world, to connect with it, to transmute, transform, and generate new information, back out into the net of Absolute Consciousness.

The body is a doorway for absorbing vast amounts of information. Sexual arousal electrifies the entire system and makes information exchange more easily available. Information is best exchanged on a physical level between two, and not three or more, because the human brain has two cerebral hemispheres that channel cross-over patterns from the subtle body, as well as the physical. It is a delicate process to integrate the subtle fibers of two individuals. We make no moral judgement about monogamy, but speak of circuit efficiency and user care. Multiple relations cause circuit interference and damage the delicate subtle wires. They also interfere with transmitting and receiving capabilities. It takes about six months to fully integrate wires between two lovers, and as long at the end of a relationship to disconnect them. So be as respectful of other's fibers as you would have them be respectful of your own. And be as respectful of your own fibers as you would the fibers of the most precious computers.

Through the body, two men can access vast amounts of information from each other. The degree of spiritual work two men have done, the amount of soul information and universal awareness they have realized will determine how much of the information exchange will be conscious, and how much will be subconscious, crossing over as a surge of energy, feeling, perhaps as heat, or tingling.

There are numerous access patterns two men can use to consciously exchange soul information. As humanity evolves, lovers will want to share more information with each other. As humanity evolves, as people become more whole, it will be understood why this exchange is important. But even now, if two lovers use these patterns but are not fully aware of the information exchange, it will still be exchanged, perhaps to become conscious later, to surface in dreams, in visions, in the midst of meditation.

Access Pattern Number One

You live more than one life in one body, in different times, or at the same time, on Earth and for some, on other worlds. All the information about these other lives is stored in the subtle body and can be accessed through the physical body.

Often new lovers have the feeling that they have known each other before. The following access pattern will help you tap into the memories of your shared lives. While the information is available for all of them, it is useful to begin by asking for and focusing on the lives where you have any unfinished business, so that it can be worked through, so that you can get down to the work you are trying to do in the present. Sometimes this information will clear the way for a long relationship by removing prior obstacles, but for others, this information will help to complete work from the past so that you can go on to other, more vital relationships. Even if this information does not become conscious, it will be exchanged, so be sure you want to open this window before you attempt this pattern.

You may want to do this at the same time, or take turns doing it. Deepen yourself into a state of expanded awareness. Use whatever method works for you, or become aware of your breath and your intention to become more aware. Let yourself feel that you are drifting into a dream. But the dream will be the recalling of another time and place when you have been together.

Partner One:

Sit at your partner's side and hold him in your arms. Rock him gently and synchronize your breathtaking with his. When he is breathing slowly, place your dominant hand around his balls. Place the fingers of your other hand on the back of his head, lightly squeezing the bump at the top of his neck, the occipital protuberance. This position, along with your intention, will activate memories of the past. Gently rock the point on the back of his head to awaken his memories. If he isn't seeing or sensing anything, move your hand from his balls to his cock and when he is aroused, slowly slide it up and down to make adjustments, then bring it back to his balls. Although you may not see or feel the past as clearly as your partner, you will also sense where he is going as he shares his journey with you. Later you can reverse positions and journey yourself.

Partner Two:

Sit with your eyes closed in your partners' arms. Synchronize your breathing with his. When he shifts his hands to your balls and the back of your head, go deeper into your consciousness, inviting images of the past to surface, from lives that the two of you share. Feelings, pictures may flash before you. At a certain point a picture or feeling will "click" with you and you can deepen into it. Start by reporting what you see and feel, letting the information unfold like a movie. Sense the resonance between who you both are now and who you are watching. Let your partner know when you are ready to return. You can do this to awaken memories of lives you shared, or you can use it to connect to specific stuck places. For example, if you are afraid of water and don't know why, as your partner rocks the back of your head, ask your deepest self if anything from your past lives has caused it.

Access Pattern Number Two

It is useful and interesting to know about past lives. They show us more of who we are, and allow us to do deep healing work, release work. But our primary focus is in this life, this body, this time and place. We come into each life with certain abilities and desires. Each life has its own set of purposes, its own necessities. We do not live in a society that supports our connection to our soul and soul purposes. We forget so easily why we are here and who we are. The tools we often use to help remember—drugs, alcohol—do not work as we would like them to. Often we get overly involved in other people's purposes as a way of forgetting that we are not sure of our own, especially with lovers. But we can connect to our own inner selves, to gifts we carry in our souls, and the spiritual work we came into this life to engage in. The following access pattern is designed to facilitate the process of self-knowing.

Partner One:

Sitting next to your partner, or cradling him in your lap, take the thumb and fingers of your dominant hand and spread them apart so that you can touch his nipples, creating a bridge between them. Cup and cradle the back of his neck with your other hand, rocking it very gently and very slowly. Move your thumb and fingers on his nipples in the slowest, smallest clockwise motion you can make.

Partner Two:

Your lover is touching you. Close your eyes, become a part of the rhythm of your breath. Let your body fill with light and know that the position of your lover's hands is a physical pattern that can help you bring up into your conscious mind the reasons you came into his life, and the things you can do to help move closer toward satisfying those purposes. Know that this pattern connects inner fibers that can stimulate the deepest parts of your creativity, if you are stuck in your life and in need of new purposes, new visions. Let pictures, words, feelings surface in your mind. Let them unfold like a flower seen in a film, speeded up as it blossoms. See how the things you think of as obstacles can be turned into creative challenges. See how you fit into the world in your uniqueness, see how you bring something into physicality that never existed before, something new and precious bridging physical and subtle realms.

Everything that exists is in a continuous process of change and rebirth. This pattern can help you tune into that energy, to fill your life with meaning and purpose. And you can use it to deepen into the sense of purpose that has brought you together with your lover, the work you need to do together, the work you can do for the human community. Whenever you feel disappointed with yourself, whenever you feel stuck, you can use this pattern to transform that place. Or if you're in the midst of incredible change, or so busy that you lose sight of what it's all about, use this pattern also.

Access Pattern Number Three

It's one thing to have spiritual visions, and another one to fulfill them in the world. One of the biggest problems people have in a world that tends to deny spiritual vision is that once you open up to it, you can get disconnected from the world, get spacey. The next pattern is designed to awaken practical, grounding visions that will help you to attain your spiritual purposes in a world that so strongly needs them.

Partner One:

Place the hand you use less on your partner's abdomen, between his navel and pubic bone. Bring his feet together and grab his big toes with your other hand, wrapping your fingers around them. It's best if he is flat on his back.

Partner Two:

Breathe deeply and slowly for a minute or two. Then let your breath breathe itself. Focus on your life and work in the world. See the world as a nurturing and supportive place. See your place in it as a necessary and important cog in the working of the world, however small a cog it seems to you. See what you came into physicality to accomplish, and look down all the avenues of the physical world to see the ways that you can pursue and accomplish them. See your spiritual work as a dance in the world.

Use this pattern to help you access specific and very practical information about jobs, people, places, times to do certain things, and ways to do them. For example, if you are going on a job interview, use this pattern to go through a dress rehearsal of what you will say and show and do there. If you are stuck in a job, having work conflicts, looking for a new job or a different vocation, use this pattern to support you in your changes. You may want to move from the last pattern to this one to ground yourself in Earth realities.

Access Pattern Number Four

It's exciting and wonderful to be opening up to these kinds of experiences. But sometimes you will find that you're suffering from information overload. You may want to go back to the safety and comfort of your old way of being in the world. Or you may be delighted with the changes, but feel like you're in the middle of a kaleidoscope, with everything glittering but nothing to hold it all together. The pattern that follows is for integration. It allows the information to exist without fear. Human life on Earth changes quickly, and this pace will quicken even more in the coming years. This pattern is a good one for rising to the complexity of life without losing your center. It helps to integrate new experiences and information, and will strengthen your sense of self.

The best way to do this pattern is for Partner One to lie on his back, and the lover looking for integration to be lying on top of him, face up. If this position is uncomfortable or impossible, it can be done on your side, belly to back, with Partner Two in front, or with Partner Two lying down and Partner One sitting beside him.

Partner One:

Take your favored hand and cup your palm around your lover's balls, with your thumb and index finger in a ring around the base of his penis. Your erection can be placed between your lover's legs. With your hand, reach around so that your fingers and thumb are bridging your lover's nipples. Feel as you hold your lover that energy is flowing between your hands, charging him and facilitating his process.

Partner Two:

Feel your breath as your lover touches you. Close your eyes and move into a feeling of support, comfort and protection. Feel your lover's love fill you and strengthen you. Move into the sense of wholeness that starts to rise up in you. Feel the breath in your body moving your abdomen in and out. Know that that rhythm in the center of your body is the beginning of your feeling centered again. See and feel and hear the way the diverse bits of information swirl you and begin to arrange themselves into a supporting structure, just as birds take bits of grass and wisps of string and shape them into a nest. Know that all of the information you have discovered, created, absorbed, is the beginning of a new mental, spiritual, practical consciousness. Feel yourself at home in this new state, and see how your life extends itself out from there.

Access Pattern Number Five

We have talked about love and lovers, we have talked about love itself as the spiritual exchange of cosmic information. We have talked about love as if it were easy. But most of you know how terrifying love and intimacy can be, especially for two men carrying guilt, shame, fear and the cultural belief that two men cannot be in a loving and intimate and enduring relationship. Part of you knows that to love and be loved is a natural part of your beingness. But, how do you get to that place when you carry such negative information about yourself, probably supported by all the relationships that did not "work out." You need to talk, to do healing work, therapy, body work, whatever you are drawn to. The more often you do the ritual outlined earlier, the closer you will become. But sometimes the fear will remain, the belief that you cannot love or be loved. This pattern will deepen your connection, open your hearts, and let love flow freely.

Partner One:

Hold your lover in your lap with your arms around him. Hold him so that you can feel each other's heart beating. Place your non-dominant hand on his chest, palm over his heart. Take your dominant hand and slip it between his legs and up to the base of his spine, so that your palm is lying flat on his sacrum. Open your heart and let the love your feel for him flow through your hands and into his body, to bless him and heal him.

Partner Two:

You are held and comforted. Feel your heart beating, feel your breath. Know that deep within your body love lies waiting. Feel your heart open. Feel your lover's love wash through you and enter every cell. Feel love rise up in you like a bird from its nest. You are filled with love now. The sacred rises up in you, in both of you, the song, the light, the breath. From sacrum, sacred bone, heart-shaped bone, to your heart itself. You are filled with love, and you are loved.

Access Pattern Number Six

How can you ground your love in your bodies when you are living in a world that has not embraced you? What can you do to support your love so that the world will not unbalance you? This access pattern is designed to do that, to ground and anchor your love.

Partner One:

You can do this pattern sitting or lying down. Take your cock in your dominant hand. Feel in the center of your heart all the love that you feel for your partner. Let it fill your heart and spread out from there to every cell in your body. Now take your feet and place them on your lover's chest, right above his heart, and send your love out of the bottoms of your feet into his body.

Partner Two:

Place yourself in a position where your lover can put his feet on your chest right over your heart. Each time that he exhales, breathe in his love for you with a deep inhalation. Draw his love into your heart and pull it down from there into your genitals. Hold your own cock in the hand you do not generally use to masturbate with. Let his grounded love spread through you to every part of your body. Receive it and hold it and breathe it deeply in, to sustain you in a world that is wobbling on its axis.

Access Pattern Number Seven

Unlike other patterns, where you and your lover access energy and information from and for each other, this is a pattern designed to beam out the love and devotion you and your lover share, into the energy grid that connects all of humanity. This is also a pattern designed for the earth and the heavens to access energy and information from you.

Both Partners:

Sit back to back with your lover. Breathe together. As you inhale, draw energy up into your body from the earth, then down into your body from the sky. Alternate heaven and earth with each breath, feeling that you are deeply connected to the universe in this way.

Place one hand on your hearts and with the other hand caress and stroke your cocks. Feel, as you do this, that the love you have for each other fills your bodies, fills the space around you, and with each exhalation, pours out into the energetic web that connects all of humanity, pours out into the heavens and the earth. Back to back, together, you create a vast and luminous column of light, that extends deep into the center of the earth, and miles up into the sky.

Know as you do this that your love is needed by the universe. Know that your love is needed by the full tribe of humanity. Know that you are entering your life into the collective unconscious so that all men who love men can tap into it, be enriched by it, be healed by it. Know that when you do this, you enter your love into humanity's collective memory banks, and support gayness in being accepted and cherished by all of humanity.

Access Pattern Number Eight

When you and your partner are open to information and open to the universe, then you can travel together to other planets, the stars, and to other realms of consciousness.

Partner One:

Lie on your stomach and know that you are like a bird, like a magic carpet. You are the one in this pattern who energetically allows movement to happen. Feel your breath, feel your heartbeat, and begin to move through dreamtime. Travel out on your breath now. Let images and feelings wash through you. Whisper them up to your partner as he rides your back.

Partner Two:

Lie on top of your lover with your erect cock between his legs. You are the pilot now, you are the one who will steer you both in your shared journey in consciousness. Feel your breath, feel your heartbeat, and let yourself rise on your lover's breathing. Guide him now, through the way you ride his body, steering him with your cock through the dreams and visions he whispers to you as you fly. Drift together in consciousness dreaming, soar high into the universe of spirit together, expanding until you are vast and wise.

Love Is the Doorway
to Transformation

Love is an energy frequency that permeates the universe. It is the subtle light the physical world emerged from. Love binds all things together. Anyone can reach it, everyone will find it. The heart is love's spinning wheel. All you have to do is find a single strand and start to spin.

Love lives in the heart of everyone. It is that spark which animates all life. Not even the heart of the fiercest mass murderer is altogether lacking in that quality, however buried under wounds, fears, lies and scars it might be. And you, how hard has it been for you to turn inward to find that light? No, you look first for that light in other people, when silently it always burns within.

Find the inner light first, and you will never feel alone again. Touch that inner light and let it glow inside, and you will begin to attract to your side others who have found that sacred inner place. The work of love is the only work there is. The work of love is that which binds all worlds together. And no one is born who has no part in this spiritual endeavor. No one exists, in bodies as you know them, in bodies of subtle matter, no one exists who is not born to be weaving, weaving love from within, weaving it into the strands of other hearts, other beings, all the world.

Feeling love, touching love, weaving it, is that which makes for change. Love is the doorway to any and all transformation.

Whoever denies this denies their own work too. Any guide or teacher who draws lines of exclusion, saying these or those among you have no place in the glorious world we can create, that person is speaking out of their own wounds. Have compassion for them, even if they call you evil, or if they deny the light that burns inside you.

The heart of the world itself, the heart of that being you call Earth, is filled with endless love. Reach into it, weave into it. Feel the amber strands of Earthlight rising up, spiraling round the globe, and weave yourselves into it. Weave it, spin it out. Join all life together in amber glowing Earth threads. This is holy work to do in meditation, grounding love in matter, making it holy again. For all partake of Earthness, in the air, through food, through touch. All bodies rise up from Earth as spirits emerge from love itself, eternal.

The work of love between men is holy, the work in community and the work of two together. The brain is made for two-together loving. And through that kind of loving, love is spun out to the world.

For too long love has been denied to men together, love, tenderness, caring. For too long the love between men has been unspoken, and only the outer form, the dance of sex, has remained. Sex is sex when only bodies dance it. But when the heart joins in, then sex is sacred. Sex made holy is that through which two can channel love out to the world. Sex made holy is that through which two connect to the origin of the world itself.

There is no one born who cannot love or be loved. Some do not believe this. But love is in the hearts of all. And when a man finds this inside, he is lovable to all but those who fear love. It is easier to find this inner love than you think. All you need to do is sit quietly and feel your heart beating. Then, turn your attention inward, and see/feel a tiny flickering golden light in the center of your heart. That is love. The more you turn to it, the brighter it will glow. The more you turn toward it, the more you weave outer strands of love into it. For the flame is a strand of love, the end of a strand—your strand. And no one is born who is not one of love's weavers.

It is time for men to gather together in communities and celebrate the love that two can share together. To make public this love is to establish loving strands to the community, so that the love two generate can be woven outward. Each public celebration is a blessing to lovers and to community. It is not the same for two men to be joined together as it is for two women or a man and a woman. It is not the same, nor is it different. In love being shared, it is identical. In bodies and frequencies being different, that which rises up from it is not the same. And the human community needs all the colors of loving that its genders allow. The human fabric needs all the colors woven in. The spiritual heart needs all colors, in order to transform human life on this planet, in order to begin the era of universal connection.

Gather in a circle, inside or outside. Gather in a circle of family and friends, to celebrate the love that two men share. Bless them in the center of the circle, and be blessed by their love. And in your communities, make loving circles to welcome those who are ready to say out loud that they are gay—gay shamans, gay artists, gay healers, gay planetary transformers. Make circles to support the end of relationships, and to celebrate the lives and passing of those who have died. Gather in circles and let your spirits connect you. Join hands, make sounds, make music, dance, share your visions. In gathering together, much that is ancient and much that is possible will be remembered and revived.

The sacred redefines itself. The world is changing. Nothing will be as it was before. Everything will be light-filled, love-filled, holy. For you have chosen to be born in an extraordinary time. When since the coming of the ice has humanity been so deeply challenged, or so capable of growth? Where once the planet itself might have destroyed you, you turn your hand against the planet. But it is time now to forgive the planet its challenges, its trials. You have used them and grown through them. You have reached a level of consciousness where you are able to communicate with those of us who are discarnate, and able to communicate with your siblings in a different frequency of sentience on the planet Earth: the dolphins and the whales. And sentient beings on countless other worlds rejoice in your having arrived at this place after thousands of years of preparation and self-education.

Rejoice in these changes. Rejoice in what is possible in this coming age. You participate in it, you have worked to create it. The work of all your past lives has brought you to this place, as humans, as men, as gay men. And we who are discarnate, guides, friends, Earth ancestors, we rejoice in these changes, in this weaving of the sacred into every aspect of your lives.

Now is the time. You are the shapers. Our blessings go out to you, our hearts and our love. So let us all rejoice in this together. In circles of love rippling out through space and time. Rippling out into the world that rises out of spirit. Rippling back to the source of all that is—to love itself.

Part Three:
Priests of Father Earth
and Mother Sky

The Mysteries of Loving

Everything that is rises up into beingness from out of the loving heart of Infinite Oneness. In a world of two genders, and in beings with brains of two hemispheres, this Infinite Oneness is perceived in dual forms. On worlds of three or more genders, of one or no genders, Infinite Oneness is perceived through the filter of threeness or fourness or fiveness or fluid one or allness.

You, who are beings of a two-fold world, perceive the Great Oneness as Goddess and God, as female and male. For so long you have seen the Earth itself, and nature, as female, as Mother. And like a mother, who gives without hesitation, the Earth has given, and you have taken. So too for thousands of years you have seen the sky, the heavens, as male, the domain of God and gods, strict in their laws, severe in their judgements of goodness and worth. But, all that is, is One—both female and male. And in the dance toward balancing your inner selves you must also seek to find the balance in the world outside yourselves. So of Earth, it is time to see it in its maleness, not as abundant giver, but as being with limits. And of sky, the time has come to know it as female, as well, compassionate and loving, embracing of all.

In everything you know and do and feel, both male and female are present. In woman there is man, in man there is also woman. When any two come together in loving, four are present, the inner and the outer, two women and two men. All is a balance, all moves toward balancing. When two come together in love who are both men, two inner women are also present. This pattern of energy generates certain connections, to movement, toward archetype, toward Oneness itself. Outwardly male, two men together cause to rise up into consciousness the forgotten powers of the Father aspect of the Earth. Inwardly female, two men together cause to spread out into consciousness the forgotten wisdom of the Mother aspects of the sky, of the heavens. So in their loving, two men together are priests of future/ancient altars. So in their loving, two men together are serving to bring human consciousness to a place of cosmic balance in the heart of loving Oneness.

In ancient times the whole of the human community knew the meanings of the mysteries of loving, of that which gives spirit form and gives form to spirit. In their great tribal convocations, the people sat in giant circles. The women who loved women sat in the north, and the north was seen as the place of stable, silent power. The men who loved men sat in the south, and the south was seen as the place of needed changes, of future direction. In the east sat those women who loved men and men who loved women, who were old enough to bring children into the world, who were participating in their nurturing. Across from them in the west sat the men who loved women and the women who loved men, who were living in transition, having taken spiritual vows, different in body and powers than the average people, or moving toward dying. The axis of north and south carried one energy, while the path from east to west carried another energy. Together, the four stations and the two energies held the human tribe together. And in those days, when the Ice was thick, the people also sat in communion with those who had died and those who never lived in bodies. Seers and speakers gave vision and voice to those beyond the physical world. And those in the physical world gave shape and form to the hopes and the dreams of those who were non-physical.

All was in balance then, female and male, incarnate and discarnate. The human community felt and knew its place in the heart of the Oneness. But as the ice receded the human world began to change. Images and archetypes changed. Internal needs to know the physical world that could not express themselves when ice covered much of the planet began to rise up into consciousness. Humanity made choices then that it is in the process of completing, and now, ten thousand years later, another cycle of human consciousness begins. Male and female move into balance again. Incarnate and discarnate begin to communicate again. Not as it was, but in a new form; the ancient circle of the full community of humans rises into consciousness. Not as it was, but in a new form; the community of men who love men remembers its purpose and its powers, and begins to use them consciously, as part of the planetary healing that every one of you participates in. For no one is alive in this time who does not have a part in this great healing. No gay man is alive now who has no share in the great mysteries that begin to reveal themselves.

The mysteries of Father Earth and Mother Sky are not the same as the mysteries of Mother Earth and Father Sky. They are not the same, nor are they a reversal, anymore than a woman is a reversal of a man or a man the reversal of a woman. This can be seen on the genetic level. Women carry chromosomes labeled X and X. But men do not carry Y and Y. The mysteries of gender are not about opposition, but about connection. Y reaches out, but what connects is X, is shared femaleness. One of the mysteries that all gay men share is that we have easier access to female energy as well as male. When two men come together in their loving, the two unseen women within them come together also. And this coming together of woman and woman, in man and man, generates an energy that makes the female powerful.

The mysteries of Father Earth and Mother Sky are not the same as the mysteries of Mother Earth and Father Sky. Both are needed, both are necessary, both are reflections of the fullness of Earth and Sky as they rise up from Infinite Oneness. When the creator and ruler of the universe is seen as Mother and not Father, all is present in Her embrace. There is no separation between spirit and matter, for She births the universe from Her body. And there is no separation between the world and humanity, between women and men, or between the different patterns of loving.

When two men come together in loving to the shrine of Father Earth and Mother Sky they will partake of ancient rites that reflect the eternal nature of who they are as a people, that were celebrated by their forefathers in the days of your ancient temples. Your shared inner female is reflected outward as Mother Sky, and the outer male is honored as the embodied spirit of Father Earth. You celebrate as scouts, as flute players, as shamans and as hunters, who carry the wisdom and power of Father Earth in your loving. Dancing on the body of Earth, radiant in the clear heaven's light of your cosmic Mother, you embody the love of Oneness, the mysteries of Oneness.

Spirits attend you, guides, Earth ancestors and angels. On every level you are connected to someone. You are not alone. Often you expect from embodied lovers the same constancy and love you feel unconsciously from your guides and angels. When you learn to sense your non-physical companions you can stop expecting unconditional love from lovers, and begin to share and celebrate the joys and pleasures of love that are possible on the physical plane and nowhere else.

From before birth all of you choose guides and angelic companions who will be with you throughout your life. We come to you in dreams and visions, and you may know us as the still, small, inner voice you call your conscience. We too partake of the energies that manifest as gay on your world. When you open to us, you expand the community of loving to the subtle planes.

For so long people have thought that a loving relationship was of importance only to the two who came together, to their families and friends. But any two who come together in love participate in the world and contribute to it. Love is not just a private matter. Among the questions to ask each other, in addition to, "How do we make each other feel?" is, "What do we give to the world?" For any two men who come together in a loving relationship create and generate an energy that can be used to heal the world and move it through the coming changes to a time of light and love and spiritual freedom. In touch, in loving, a vibration is created, a song, a chant. This is the sound of two flutes playing. And the power of that song is two together moving through consciousness, two together pursuing the essence of life, two together healing. Any two can heal. Every two men together bound by love can use their energy to be gay healers.

Dying is a choice. Living is a choice. When you connect to the spirit in you, you can make these choices consciously. Then you will know yourself not as a victim of your life, but as its creator.

If someone is in need of healing, two lovers, sit on either side of them. Create a circle of healing around the one who needs it. Feel that the waves of energy you generate wash into them, opening and awakening in them the core of who they are and why they came to be born. Feel this energy wash through them. Feel it move into the deepest places of their intentionality. Feel it awaken in them their purest purpose, clearest desire, holiest choices. Sit on either side of them, sit one at the foot and one at the head. Use the power of your loving to embrace them. Become the priests of Father Earth that you are, and embody his forms and his energies. Become the world as part of your healing power. Use the powers of the world to inspire. For you are healers in the world, in a world that needs deep healing. And all who live upon this world both participate in the healing and require it.

And if you have not a love in a physical body, does this stop you, gay healer, from doing the work at hand? Just reach out to one of your non-physical companions. Feel the same power of connecting, the same connection of heart. For we live on many levels, love on many levels, heal on many levels also.

In this day and in this time a new tribe of gay men is being born. Not as it was, this tribe of many clans, but being born into what it will be. Still a tribe of dreams, it is you who father the tribe that all future generations of gay men will be born into. Birth it from your loving hearts with all the tenderness and compassion that the world you were born into did not provide. Love it with the passionate heart of a devoted father, generous and strong. Know that what you do and say and create now is the legacy you leave behind to the gay men who will follow you. Know that the gay tribe you create may be one into which you will be born again, in a future incarnation. Sit quietly and allow yourselves to dream. Dream, write, talk, sing to each other all the stories of how gay life should be, could be, will be if you plant the seeds to grow it now. You are birthing the gay tribe of tomorrow. Come together in groups. Sit quietly and join all your energies together. Remember the past and its gay tribes as you remember the future. Come together in circles, gay priests of Father Earth and Mother Sky. Sit quietly and bring the sacred back into your lives. When you reclaim the sacred, priesthood is restored. Then, the energy of Mother Sky embraces you and offers blessings. Then, the energy of Father Earth rises up through you to empower you, to cleanse you. Then you move in perfect balance with the changes in the living heart of Oneness. Then you move in perfect balance with the aspects of your inner selves.

Sit in circles and feel the presence of we who surround you come close and embrace you. Sit in circles and feel the energies of all gay men who ever were and ever will be come close and sit beside you. For what you are is the expression of a weaving of vibrations. And wherever there is humanness, these vibrations will appear. On every world, on every plane these vibrations appear, rising up from the living heart of Infinite Oneness. Always with a different face and yet always the same.

Sit together in your circles, join hands, open your hearts. Feel the energy that you generate when you do this. Feel the waves of energy you create wash out from the circle and spread out into the world. Let that circle carry joy and hope and wisdom and love with it. Know that energy touches everyone on this planet when you join together. Beam out love, then joy, then peace. Feel waves of that energy touch all the members of the greater human tribe, touch those who know and love you and touch those who fear and hate you. Build bridges of love in the world of greater humanness, bridges to your enemies as well as to your friends. Know that in your hearts and minds exists the capacity to change the world. Own this healing power, gay men, and use it. Stand proudly in the world as men. Sit together in your circles strongly, gently, lovingly. Know that what makes a man a Man is an open heart. Know that what makes a gathering of people a tribe is a common dream, a common song, a common heart. Be heartful in your circles, men. Reach out to each other not with open, judging eyes but with open, caring hearts. Reach out your hands in greeting and lightly touch each other's hearts. Know that what cannot be seen is ever-present, and what cannot be seen can be felt and loved and known.

Be Priests of Father Earth and Mother Sky, as gay men have been for ten thousand years. Love the Earth and work to heal it. Know that this work is a part of your gayness. Move freely in the world of plants and trees, finding friends there, comrades, allies. For your energy can be strong as a forest of deeply rooted trees, shimmering in the sunlight, whispering, sheltering, mighty. And remember the ancient/future ways in which God was also known once as the Mother. Feel her power and claim it as your own. Be loving mothers to each other, nurturing and comforting and strong. Let the world that is changing include you with its changers. Own the power to heal and the power to renew.

One day on your world there will be no gay children born, nor straight children either. Just loving children will be born. But in this time of your history these varied patterns still function within you and need to be understood. Once the parents of the world knew about these patterns and it is time for the whole of humanity to know about them again. Speak lovingly to your families and friends about the ways that you are different and the ways that you are the same. Sit quietly in your meditations and send hope and love and knowledge to all the parents of the world and all the children, that a world can be born in which the freedom to love is always honored and the capacity to love is always rejoiced in.

What makes a woman a Woman and a man a Man is not sexuality but loving. What makes a people joyous is not what they do with their bodies but the energy that they allow to flow through them. Love is an energy. Love is that which first emerged from the heart of Infinite Oneness. Love is that from which all worlds arose and that which holds the universe together. Love is the natural frequency that the human heart exists to function on. Send love to each other and send love to the Earth.

Sit quietly, lay quietly on his body. Let love well up in your heart and fill your body. Send it out from your heart and your hands into his body, Father Earth's. For it is up fromhis body that all life has emerged here. For it is time to sit quietly and give him thanks as a part of his healing. For at the hands of human beings Father Earth has suffered deeply. But from the hands of human beings a healing can begin. Plant trees and work to end the pillaging of this planet. This is part of your function as gay priests to do this work. Move deeply into the heart of this planet and move with him. Draw up his energy into your bodies and beam it out into the world. For if you do not connect with the Earth and begin to make a healing then no healing can begin within your lives. And when you work with Earth to create a world of healing then energies will rise up from his body to renew you and to bless you. You will move with the weather and the seasons. All life will flourish here again.

Feel in your hearts and souls the joy of Mother Sky. Reawaken in yourselves again the form of God-perception that your earliest ancestors met when they reached out in spirit. Feel Goddess again as the balance and completion of what you have known for so long as male. Let these feelings and memories awaken in you, gay priests, who have for so long served her altars without remembering what it was that you were reaching toward. In this remembering is great healing. Inner and outer will come into balance, female and male, living and dying. For the body you know is only one aspect of who you are. The body is holy. The body is the soul's desire to express itself made manifest. So rejoice in yourself and your beingness. Rejoice in the powers of Infinite Oneness that allowed to rise up from the heart of Itself the great and holy mystery called life.

Today you begin to create the future. Every day you work at weaving through the world those patterns of choice that will create the future. Let the vision rise up in you of your wisdom and your power. Let the vision rise up in you of the tribes of gay men that once lived on this planet. Let the vision rise up in you of the strong and loving gay tribes of the future. See yourselves in all your beauty living fully and freely in the world. See yourselves as artists, scientists, politicians, healers, wise men, growing strong in your families, growing strong in the world. And feel the bonds between you and other gay men grow strong with loving. Feel the bonds between all of humanity grow strong with heartful loving. See the tribe of all humanity grow strong in its diversity. For in the fullness of humanity great joy and wonder will reveal itself.

In the heart of this moment you spin out the fibers of life that will become your planet's future. Weave strongly and gently and wisely, knowing there is little time to waste and yet all of eternity in which to choose.

In The Temple of Father Earth and Mother Sky

There was a time when the world was poised between the way things are now, and the way that they were then. The ice was gone. Towns and villages were being established. Men and women owned their differences and were still able to communicate with each other. The sacred places of the Mother still functioned, in groves and caves and on the tops of mountains. The Earth was honored as one of her incarnate sons. The new male gods were not yet all-powerful. People remembered the powers of women, the powers of the scouting tribes, and they tried to honor those powers at the same time as they lay down walls for villages and temples, and elevated their gods and priests and armies and kings.

Now, this was almost three thousand years after the time of Tayarti and his successors. For all of that time, tribes of gay men, pairs of gay lovers, had wandered the world of the Mediterranean, as healers and shamans and midwives for the dying. Wherever there was need of this work, among any of the people, we were there to do our chosen service. Large and small, we had hundreds of encampments, some permanent, some temporary. There we lived and loved, raised the sons that came to us, teaching them our wisdom, preparing them to find their own partners, and carry on the work. In those days, all the people honored us, cherished us, depended on us for our wisdom and our power to be connectors and balancers.

But the world was changing. The old ways were being forgotten. What made people different from each other was becoming more important than what connected them, and the need for connectors from any of the scouting tribes was becoming less and less honored. And, where not so long before all of humanity had been nomadic or seasonally nomadic, people were settling down, asserting their claims to territory that had once been free for all to wander through. Armed villages were beginning to fight to defend their boundaries, and this was especially difficult for our people and others like us, who were even more nomadic than others. As blood and birth and boundaries became a common source of power, there was less and less room in the world for tribes who came together from affinity and not from biological connection.

In those days, the ancient belief in God as Mother was being replaced by an awareness of God's Father aspects, and women's sacred powers were being questioned. So too, the old male sense of Earth was being replaced by a belief in a female Earth, as a mother without limits. Men in all tribes were taking more and more power onto themselves, beginning to pillage the earth in the process. Now, we were a people known for our ability to contain both male and female energies in one body in a state of perfect balance. And as the distance between female and male continued to grow, it became more and more difficult for people to see us in our wholeness.

It was in that time, in the north of Africa, in what is now known as Tunisia, that a group of the elders of our tribe came together at the beginning of summer, in a place called Yahl-wah-tay, Place where Animals Cross the Water. Yahl-wah-tay was a major festival gathering spot for all the people. Feeling the changes going on in the world, and sensing a danger for the people of our tribe, our elders came together in that place, to share their wisdom, their stories and their dreams. This was in the days not long after Akidrada was doing his work, healing, teaching, wandering from the north of Italy into what is now Turkey, where he died. And it was several thousand years before the building of the pyramids.

The chief of the elders in that time was a man named Kuniata. It was he who first dreamed about building a permanent temple and community in that place. In his dream he saw the first courtyard of the temple, and the walls, both inner and outer. It was he who marked out on the dirt the lines that became walls, the lines that became lodgings and healing rooms, the lines that became the inner shrine of the temple, where the men of our tribe gathered to pray, meditate, connect with each other, with the spirits of the ancestors of our tribe, and with the Oneness that connects us all.

Over the next fifty years, the men of our tribe built a temple and gathering place for our people in that valley. They called it "Nas-mahay Tal-wah-hahn," the Temple of Father Earth and Mother Sky. There, our priests were able to teach and share and preserve their ancient wisdom—for our tribe and for all the people. The memory of that first gay temple is still carried in the collective unconscious. It was a simple complex of mud-dried brick and wood and stone, with painted walls and doorways. But all the temples of our people that followed it were patterned by this first temple, in every part of the Western world, from Africa to Sweden, from Palestine to Spain.

This temple was guided by a long line of gay elders, who remembered the old ways, remembered the path of Tayarti and his followers. They remembered that we are a people who walks between male and female, between the living and the dead, between matter and spirit, between heaven and earth. They remembered the old ways, saw how much the world was changing, and sought to preserve what still lived from the past, preserve and interpret it in a way that would make sense to the people of that time. Tayarti had seen the great changes coming, he had dreamed about them, but he did not live to see them. In that time, however, at the dawn of what we call civilization, the changes were becoming real.

From Kuniata and Relag, his student and successor, a long line of elder-priests followed. In addition to the elders, many other priests lived in that temple. Some of them were healers, and much of the healing work they did was as midwives for the dying, healing people into radical transformation, no matter what stages of life they were in. In those days, when people were stuck in their lives, they worked with us in order to have a vision, to 'die' and be reborn, be renamed. Some of these priests were herbalists, some music makers, image makers, but all of them were shamans, wandering out as guides into certain areas of consciousness, as our people have done since the beginning of human time.

We may think of these people as primitive, but their spiritual culture was as advanced as our material culture is today. They understood both the physical body and the subtle bodies. Through dreams they were able to connect across great distances with other elders of our tribe, just as we do via telephones. Their chosen work was to help the people remember love and loving in a time when humanity was beginning to explore physicality, power, separation and destruction. They left behind no material artifacts. Their temples are long gone. But their story remains.

Not all the men of our tribe lived or worked in that first temple, or the ones like it that were built all over the ancient world. For those who did, there was a long period of initiation and training. Boys who felt the calling came to live in the temples when they were around 14 years old. Their training for the next seven years was in sacred music and dance, in massage, both physical and energetic, healing with herbs, tending to the dying, traveling out to the places beyond death to help connect the dying to their guides and families on the other side.

In that time, people still understood that healing energy and sexual energy are the same. So the raising of sexual energy was taught, the ways to use that energy to awaken healing and awareness in the physical body. Through different access patterns in the body, initiates could be opened up to other states of consciousness and other levels of inner wisdom. In sexual trance states they traveled to other realms and met the earth ancestors of our tribe, the gay elders who became their teachers on other planes. They were trained to take pilgrims of our own tribe to the realm that is our spiritual haven, and at death, many of them chose to join the earth ancestors and remain there as non-physical teachers. Kuniata and many of his followers remain there to this day, as powerful guides for us to listen to and learn from.

For seven years initiates would be in training with the older priests. During that time most of them paired up with another initiate, to travel the path together. At age 21, they were ready to be priests in the Temple of

Father Earth and Mother Sky, two together serving as healers, serving together around the great tree that was the living altar of the temple.

For seven years they served as priests for all the people, and as teachers of the new initiates. At the end of those seven years, from the age of 28 until their deaths, they served as elders, counselors and teachers. It was in that period of their lives that the ancient story, song and dance cycles from Tayarti and his followers were learned by heart and taught to the new priests.

At moon festivals and other sacred times, the men of our tribe who did not live in the temple came to be with the priests and novices who did. They came together there, to learn our ancient history, through stories, through music, through dance and through sacred touch. They came to bask in the power we had in our tribes, the power of love that the men and women loving tribes did not have, the power for every single member of our tribe to be the potential partner of every single other member. It was that power, that unity, which nurtured us, empowered us, made us holy and the reflection on Earth of the Greater Oneness that is the source of all that is and ever will be.

At first that temple was a great healing place for our people and for all the tribes. People came there to be ushered into power dreams. They came to understand why they were unbalanced in their bodies, minds and spirits. They came to us to be healed of those imbalances. For we were the balancing tribe for all the people. Able to draw into our bodies Mother Sky energy and Father Earth energy, we were taught by our elders to use those energies to retune other men who were not of our own tribe, to be balanced in their lives and to be healed into their dying.

But the time of clarity in Yahl-wah-tay was brief. For 26 generations the clarity remained, through 26 generations of elder-priests. But the growing into strength of what we call the patriarchy began to intrude into the workings of that temple, and all the other temples that were built after it, both our temples, and all the temples of women everywhere. We still had our work, our living altar, around which ancient tree we danced, sang, and on certain holy days, offered the seed of our bodies. But beyond the temple walls, the priests and leaders of the new gods were taking over people's lives. It did not happen overnight. It happened in different times and places in different ways. But slowly, it happened everywhere, in the West and in the East as well, that the journey to wisdom through suffering became a global art form.

No longer did all of humanity move through the world in a sacred way. In turning our focus to the physical world, we as a species created a rift between our physical body and our energy bodies. Once, living in a body on the Earth was a source of sacredness. But disconnected from the spiritual energies that come to us through our subtle bodies, people no longer felt sacred all the time. Once, every relationship between two lovers, two men, two women, a woman and a man, was a source of sacredness, a channel to

Divine energy. But in that time, humanity turned away from the doorway to sacredness that is love, and began to explore other realms of consciousness. There had been hostility between tribes before, but there had never been war. In those days, humanity invented war for the first time.

Over the centuries, as our focus on the physical world grew stronger, our collective ability to sense and move in the non-physical realms grew more restricted. Hoping to prevent a total separation between the two, the priests in our temples began to work in a new and more focused way. Where they had once helped the people to keep their energies balanced, all that was left to them was to serve the people as conduits for Divine connection. So in rooms once used for all kinds of healing work, in temples all across the ancient world, men we now call sacred prostitutes began to appear.

Instead of working together in pairs, as we had always done, our priests began to work alone. Still capable of drawing into their bodies the energies of our Divine Parents, they were able, for a time, to transmit some of that Divine energy to their partners, through sexual connection. In this we hoped to bring them nearer to the world of spirit again. This was considered holy work, yet it was only a fragment of what our holy work had been in earlier times.

For thousands and thousands of years, everyone had seen us as a people, a people with specific gifts and powers. But in those days, for the first time in human history, others were starting to see our power as coming from our sexuality, and not as coming from our peoplehood and from our inner gifts. For the first time in history, they began to see our work as about sex, and not about consciousness scouting, healing and transformation.

In a world without ice, fear of freedom forced people to contract more than the cold had ever made them contract. As a species we were not ready for freedom. As men and women drew apart, the universe itself was coming to be seen as divided between male and female—with nothing to connect them but the act of sex itself, on a personal level and on a cosmic level. For the first time in our history, our tribe was divided. Those who found it easier to connect with their femaleness had no other role available except for that of serving in the temples; while those who found it easier to connect with their maleness were excluded, forced to join the tribe of all tribes, to marry and focus their love of other men into sexual connection only.

Instead of meeting each other whole, we began for the first time to en-counter each other in our tribe in a fragmented way. For the first time, gay priests served our Divine Parents alone, and not in pairs. Men who came to the temples whenever they needed balancing in any part of their lives came only for sexual connection. As we lost our balance as a people, our temples became unbalanced. As we lost our sense of male Earth connection, as people began to see male energy as heavenly and remote from the world of the senses, our temples became goddess temples only.

In that time, to echo in their bodies the mutilation that was happening to us as a people, and to echo in their bodies the unbalanced femaleness that was being imposed on them, our sacred priests began to be castrated, to dress in women's garments, to offer in a fragmented way what little remained of our ancient powers. For the first time in human history, people began to think that gender and sexuality were the same, that men were supposed to be attracted to women only, as women were supposed to be attracted only to men. But as long as they were seen as female, it was still acceptable for other 'men' to connect with the prostitutes in our temples. And while there was ecstasy in their service, ecstasy and a sense of Divine intoxication, it is good to remember that ecstasy means 'to displace,' to be 'out of body.' For we had become a displaced, disembodied people.

Yet the word in the Bible that is translated as cultic prostitute is a word that means Holy One. This is our history, our heritage, and part of the hidden history of women. It is woven into the consciousness bands of this planet, no matter how fiercely anyone tries to erase it, no matter how they fail to understand it. We are the ones who still carry the knowledge that the body is holy, that sex is holy, that the only way that we can heal the air, the water, the land, is by loving our own and each others' bodies again, by loving the body of the planet we live on, whether we come to it as Father or Mother, by ending our displacement, by bringing love back to the places we live in—to our bodies and to the world.

In time, there were temples all around the Great Inner Sea, the Mediterranean, where men of our tribe, cut away from each other and from their own inner balance of genders, lived out the last of our powers, serving the Mother as sacred prostitutes. Alone, yet in holy service, we did what we remembered of our ancient work, in the best ways that we could. We were called Holy Ones. And yet, the holy power we had in those days was but a fragment of the powers we once had.

For a thousand years, the last of our priests served in goddess temples. Then, the powers of the male gods and their priesthood grew. Villages became cities, and cities became nations with vast standing armies. Soon, the male gods would became a male God, and even the great temples we served in would be 'cleansed' of our presence. Prophets would rail against us. The people would come to hate and fear us. What little remained of our love and power would be branded as unnatural. The sacred groves of our temples would be cut down, our living altars, cut down. The goddesses we served would be debased, their priestesses forced into virginity, then excluded from sacred service all together. As the patriarchal priesthood took over the world, there was no room for women, for men who were seen as women, no room for joy or pleasure or physical sacraments. But our energy is strong, too strong to be completely denied. And we who are born to draw in Earth and Sky for all the people, who chose to enter our tribe to express something of our inner balance in the world of form, took our ancient powers and transformed them once again.

There had always been sacred dances, trance dances, sacred singers and choruses who helped to align and connect and heal the people. This had gone on in every tribe. But in the time when the old ways were being destroyed, when our scouting powers were gone, our shamanic powers gone, it was then that men of our tribe took one of our innate powers, our ancient flute player energies, and redefined them again. No longer able to connect with each other, no longer able to serve in the temples to retune other men, we tapped into our ancient powers, and invented something new.

In ancient Greece, in the service of a new god come from the East, where our people remembered more of our old power, a new god born from the body of his father, and connected to the earth as we had been, in the service of Dionysus, we invented something new out of our ancient powers.

In the last of the groves, on the hillsides behind temples, there we created theatre. There, in a sacred way, in costumes and masks, we became goddesses and gods, heroes and heroines. We did this to preserve what is innate and true and holy in us in the best ways we could find. We did this for all the people, to align and connect and heal them. And we carried this gift to all of our people, so that they too, wherever they were, could make use of our sacred powers in the world again. For we are the people who can hold male and female equally in balance in our bodies. And we took that power, that balancing power, and we gave it back to all the people, in a new way. If we could not balance them as healers, if we could not balance them as lovers, we would balance them on stage.

The earliest plays were not about ordinary men and women. They were about gods and heroes, because the actors were trained to channel the energies of those gods and heroes from the spirit realms. The last of our priests became writers, directors, stage master shamans, who taught other men of our tribe how to draw in those energies, and how to beam them out to the people who watched them, listened to them. This was as true in the East as in the West, that men of our tribe came together in this way to serve all the people. This was in the time when women, except for the last of the priestesses and sacred prostitutes, were seen as nothing more than the possessions of their fathers and then husbands. So there were no female performers, and would not be for thousands of years. We, the men of our tribe, we carried that energy out into the world, in the only ways that the patriarchy would allow it.

And so it was in that time, that the only way the men of our fragmented tribe could find each other, to do what remained of our sacred work, was in theatres, on stages. Our loving had to be kept secret. Our power had to be kept secret. Even on stage, who we were was a secret. And even in ancient Greece, often thought of as the home of homosexuality, we could only love each other in unequal relationships, where instead of being teacher-partners, one man became the other's teacher. But still, we did our work, the work we were born to do. We built our theatres, we told the old stories in the best ways that we could, as female and male, with music and dancing, in honor of the god who was himself in balance. And if we were no longer powerful as a people, our work was.

Then as a species, we deepened further into our journey of exploration of physicality. We had no more room for joy, for pleasure. The male God demanded sacrifice and obedience. Even theatre was seen as debasing. Ancient stages were destroyed. The sacredness of our work, of what remained of our work, was once again denied. Our capacity to love was forbidden, considered evil. And this time, many of the men of our people, remembering their inner priesthood, but having forgotten any sense of our tribe, turned away from the ancient body sacraments all together, became celibate, joined new priesthoods—but still continued to teach and heal in the best ways they knew how.

Here and there, someone remembered our ancient history, in stories, in fragments. Sometimes all that was remembered was that this god had loved a mortal man, in this or that place, a long, long time ago, be he Zeus or perhaps Jesus. But even those fragments were enough to feed us in the years of forgetting. For we took our last remaining power, we took our hunter energy, and we wandered out into the wilderness of the world, hunting for ourselves, hunting for each other. At times we went so far into the wilderness of plains and cities that we lost sight of who we were and why we were there. Alone, each one of us thought himself to be the only one. For just as the world forgot, or tried to, that we exist, that we exist in a sacred way, with sacred powers meant to be used for all the people, we ourselves forgot who we are.

All over the Western world, we were tortured and burned at the stake, with witches and others who struggled to live and to remember the old healing ways. This part of our history we know, have lived with. And when we met, if we met at all, the only thing left to us was sexual connection. Nameless, faceless, in fear, in shame, in bliss, we met each other, hungering for something of our ancient selves that sex alone could never satisfy, and never will.

But some of our ancient wisdom remained in other places. When the people of Europe invaded the Americas, they found a proud and living tradition of men who remembered the balancing ways, men sometimes dressed in women's garments, men who lived their lives in a sacred way, who were sexual with other men. This was too much for the European terror merchants, who transported their life-negating inquisitions to a world still new to them. And we live in the culture they brought with them. We are a part of that 'civilization.' And yet just beneath our asphalt streets, something of the old sacredness of the peoples of this continent remains for us to connect with.

No, we did not go away. We could not. In a village, in a province, in a kingdom, in an empire, they could try to exterminate all of us—and in the next generation, their very own bodies would betray them—and give birth to us again, to us and to all the peoples of the scouting tribes. They could take away our history, destroy our sacred places, burn us, look on while disease took away our young men. But we are a part of this planet, woven into and out of its body. And, we will never go away.

We were never a people with borders and territory. We were always a nomadic people. And lost from ourselves, lost from each other, lost from history, tortured, damned and locked away, still we endured. And now, now it is time for the men of our tribe to find each other again, become a tribe again. Of ourselves, for ourselves, and for our sacred Father Earth, forgotten and longing for his sons to remember him.

Painful as it has been, we cannot regret this journey. We had to take it in order to find out who we are and what we are made of. It was part of our evolution as an incarnate sentient species. And now, having been on this journey, having seen ourselves from as far away from ourselves and from the Divine as we could get, we are ready to become ourselves again, in life, in joy, in wholeness. We are ready for the first time to be free. We are ready for the first time to hold together spirit and form, as even the wisest of our ancestors in the time of the ice could not do, who had not mastered form yet.

And we, we who have been female and male, rich and poor, of every age, region, faith, we awaken anew to who we are, all over the planet. We remember that we are a people, created by Infinite Oneness with certain gifts. We remember that we are a sacred people, a holy people. We remember that we are a wise and strong and tender people. We remember that we are hunters, and also flute players, that we are consciousness scouts, and also shamans.

Made stronger by our long and terrible journey, we come together as a people again. Together, in this time, we remember our sacred gifts, and make ready to share them with the world again. For what we are, all the rest of humanity will become. They carry the seed of life in their bodies. We carry balance in ours. They carry us in their bodies, just as we carry a scouting vision of their destiny. For in the heart of the Divine, we are one people, one great tribe. And, our common destiny—must be Dreamed Together.

Living Our Priesthood in the World

To be gay is something that begins within ourselves. It begins in our hearts, in that place that is never separate from the living heart of Infinite Oneness. To be gay is something that begins with ourselves, that finds itself mirrored back, echoed back to us by the tribe of men who love men. This tribe, our people, is a scouting tribe, a Walks-Between people, a bridge-making people, walking between men and women, between night and day, between matter and spirit, between the living and the dead.

There are many tribes in the global nation of all tribes. For so long we have defined ourselves in opposition to the great and slow moving body of the nation of all tribes itself. We have defined ourselves, and been defined, by that which seemed to be in us most different. But a tribe must define itself from within, not without. And it is not our sexual nature alone, nor its difference from the woman-and-man-loving sexual nature of the body of the global tribe that makes us different.

Often we have sought our allies among the other peoples that the larger tribes have attempted to exclude from the global nation, among tribes that are defined by blood and land ties, ethnic and racial ties. But our natural allies are not to be found among these peoples. Our natural allies are those other tribes who rise up from the main body of the people, who are not linked by generational and genetic connections, but are linked by their own separate natures. Our natural allies are the other scouting tribes.

In this time of transformation, we are not the only new/old people to be rediscovering itself, its wisdom and its power. The Blind, Deaf, Disabled and Lesbian tribes are also coming together, remembering who they are, making themselves known and asking for their rightful place in the tribe of all tribes. They too are remembering that they have a language and a culture that unite them. These are our natural allies, and now is the time for us to seek deeper connections with these other peoples, who emerge from the main body of the tribe, define themselves from within, and scout out the consciousness terrain, not just for themselves, but for all of humanity.

Each scouting tribe explores a different direction of human awareness and potentiality. Taken together, the work of all the scouting tribes creates for the main body of the people a picture of what it is and where it is going. This is holy work, however much we ourselves, and the global tribe, have forgotten it or denied it.

In this time of crisis, it is the scouting people who hold out, by our very natures, the deepest vision of healing and peace that is possible for the entire global nation. For a scouting tribe gathers itself up from every other tribe, ethnic, racial, religious, regional, from every age and location, and finds common ground to connect. The more strong and public these scouting tribes become, the more clearly the capacity deepens for *all* peoples to come together across geographic, political, historical and enemy lines. This information, the capacity to connect, is entered into the collective unconscious, for all peoples to make use of. So it is not by our nature alone that we make a difference in the world, but by our actions, our thoughts, in our coming together as a tribe.

Once every tribe had its seers, its healers, its shamans. But the scouts in consciousness were considered the shamans for the great nation of all the people. This was in the end of the Ice Ages, so you may not think that this has anything to do with life today. But, what was established in the collective unconscious then, remains true for us and for all the people.

In those days, the Deaf tribe spoke a universal language of hands, and were global ambassadors and information carriers. They were also able to hear the inner word, and were the truth tellers for the people. The Blind Tribe were consummate healers, bards, judges and historians for each tribe, and because they could see beyond, they were also the theoretical physicists of their time. Each Disabled tribal member bent out beyond the shared reality of the main body of the tribe. They were the guardians of planetary and weather information, hunting, planting and astronomy. Our Lesbian sisters were known as the Holds Together people, for they were connected to the primal creative energy of the Mother, as guardians of the animals, of birth and growth and keepers of the rites of passage for all the people.

In those days, shamans used drum, rattle, chant, a flickering fire in a darkened cave, fasting, mind altering substances, to make the shift into other realms of consciousness. But we have all been shamans in different lives. And while drums and chants can root us in our history, we do not need them to travel any longer. The tools, the path, the ways to make shifts are simple to learn, to remember.

Imagine a time when we and all the scouting tribes find our rightful places in the tribe of all tribes. Imagine a time when we will have—not our own states, our own nations, but everywhere on the globe—centers, retreats, encampments in the midst of all the other peoples, places where we can go to heal, commune, remember and create, places where we can do our scouting work, for ourselves and for the whole people.

Imagine this world. This world where any boy growing into manhood, who knows that his heart is a heart tuned toward men, can travel freely to one of these centers, with the blessings of the family that brought him into the world, there to learn about himself, his tribe, his heritage. In safety, in beauty, in love, he will be taken into the tribe. In his own time, his own way, whole and strong.

One day there will be thousands of these centers all over the Earth. There we will deepen into ourselves as the Walks-Between People, so that we can share what we have learned about the places between night and day, female and male, body and spirit, with all the world. Each of these centers will be connected both through an energetic web and a technological and informational one. Thus, the men in each will be attuned to the others, in harmony with each other, communicating with each other, working and net-working, loving and healing and dreaming together. For in dreams, in dream-ing together, a tribe renews itself and remembers its most ancient roots. And a people that does not know its roots cannot live, anymore than a tree can live without its roots.

Many of our religions have taught us that through spiritual practices we will be able to escape from the Earth plane. The paradoxical truth however, is just the opposite. In meditation we do not escape from this plane. Rather, we merge our consciousness with the planet, so that we know reality, know the cosmos, in the fluid, vast and expansive way that Earth does.

In our encampments, in our new communities, we will gather together and deepen consciously into the loving embrace of our Earthly Father. Alone and with others we will know as he knows, feel as he feels, see as he sees. And we will carry this awareness back to the peoples of all the other tribes. We will write about it, sing about it, paint about it, heal from this knowing, love from this knowing, move through the world with this knowing in every cell of our bodies. For no one, sage, saint or angel, can know the cosmos without knowing it through a body.

Whatever plane it exists on, the body is the vehicle through which infor-mation flows. And as we are a people who Walk Between matter and spirit, between wise one and fool, between day and night, between woman and man, we are the people who will bring this truth back to the world. For we cannot separate the healing of the body of the Earth from the healing that is needed in our own bodies and in our relationship to them.

The work in community is the life-blood of a tribe, its reason, its pur-pose. The work in community is what links together matter and spirit, past and future, what links together individuals, lovers, the tribe and the world. The work in community is sacred, ceremonial, the gathering point in time and space for all levels of the tribe, physical and non-physical.

Our tribe will create for itself many rituals. A Coming-In ritual, for those men of any age who are ready to enter our tribe. A Stands-Proud ritual, to bless and honor anyone in our tribe. A Finds-Himself ritual, for any man in need of nurturance, support and healing. A Walks-Beside ritual, to consecrate the union of lovers, and a Walks-Separately ritual, to support the un-raveling of a union. Let there be a Turns-Away ritual, for those men who have loved men who chose to activate the fibers that will support them in loving women. And a Walks-With-the-Ancestors ritual, to celebrate the lives of those men who have untied themselves from their physical bodies, to support them in their journey of transformation.

Our people carries its history with it. This information is available to everyone on the planet, just as it is to anyone who carries our resonance pattern with him. From the time that he is floating in his mother's womb, a man who loves men is tapping into the collective history of our tribe. The roots of our history are sacred, but much of our history has been painful, and that information is stored in the memory banks too. Part of the work of our tribe in this time is to make new entries in the memory banks in order to heal ourselves, our ancestors, and our tribal heirs. What follows is a ceremony to release the pain still carried in our history, so that no man born into our tribe will step into the world with this pain in his fibers.

Sit together in a circle. All ceremonies begin in a circle, for whereas birds fly from place to place in a triangle, the perfect pattern for human beings to fly from state to consciousness state is in a circle. In the center of your circle there can be an altar of fire, water, sacred objects, or empty space. Hold hands around the altar you have created, breathe together, feel your hearts beating together. Then create a web of energy that connects you all. Know that you are safe and woven together.

Now, draw energy up from Father Earth, up through the tip of your spine. Fill your body with his amber light. Then draw energy down through the top of your head from Mother Sky. Hold her sparkling light in your body and be full with it. Feel your power, Walks-Between Men. Know that heaven and earth come together in your bodies.

Then, invite our ancient ancestors to join you in an outer ring of this circle, the gay Earth Ancestors of the four directions, the spirit guides of our tribe, our ancient teachers. Feel them gathering around you, bathed in silver light. Next, invoke the angels who attend our tribe, and feel them also join your circle, in an outermost ring, golden and shimmering, their wings wrapped around you all.

Breathe together, tone together. Let sound pour forth from your bodies. This sound will align the circles into a unified energy field. In the silence after the sound, feel a powerful pulsing of love wash through you, from hand to hand, from ring to ring. Fill your body with love. Breathe it into all the sad and wounded parts of you, still suffering from living in a world where our capacity to love is not yet honored. Let this love be a healing, a healing in every thought, in every cell. Then, send love out. Send this love to all the others in your circle. Send this love out along the energy strands that connect your gathering to all the other gatherings of our people. Send that love out to the world, to all the people, all the other living beings, to the planet itself, our loving Father. Send this love out into the web of information that surrounds the planet, that carries its history, that carries our history. Know that when you do this you retune the collective memory, enter this love in, and transmute the pain. And send this love out to our Mother the Sky, so that she who birthed us can share in the joy of our loving.

When the circle is alive with love, rippling out in every direction, invite into the center of the circle all the men who loved men who have ever lived, suffered, and are still in need of healing, friends and lovers who have died of AIDS, friends and lovers going back through time. See the generations of men who have been tortured and killed for their love, or kept that love hidden away in fear, feel their spirits step into your circle, be embraced and cleansed, baptized and healed by it.

Lastly, when you have made this healing for our gay fathers and grandfathers, feel the spirits of all the gay men not yet born, our spiritual sons and grandsons, rising up from the center of the circle. Invite them into your loving circle, to be welcomed and blessed. Let them know that they will not be born alone, nor grow into their man-loving beauty alone, as so many of us did. See them born in love, growing in love, strong and standing tall in the world. See them rise up from the circle and travel out into the world, carrying our love with them to every part of the planet.

Sit in silence, alive with love. Make sound again, deep body sound, wordless chant. Use the sound to send, solidify and seal your love. And as you are ready, bring yourselves back to the moment. Renewed. Inhale together. Exhale together. Step out of your circle.

Once there were clearly established sacred times and sacred places, but all of that becomes fluid now. This ceremony can happen anywhere, at any time. However, in the days of the ice, people came together on the night before the full moon, the night of the full moon, and the night after it, when they wanted to transmit energy in the world. The days and nights around the full moon are still good times to gather.

We are a Walks-Between people, between female and male, matter and spirit, night and day. So, too, what binds our tribe together will come not only from the work we do in the world, but also from the work we do at night.

In the Ice Ages, when gay shamans needed to convene and communicate with each other across long and frozen wastes—they met in their dreams. Wherever they were, these sons of Tayarti came together in the same dream places, to talk, to share wisdom, to pool their energies. They had several different meeting places. But when they had sacred work to do, they met in the Sacred Men's Shrine of Kandayata.

You too can connect this way. Whether you sleep alone or with others, you too can move across the web that connects our tribe. You too can go on a pilgrimage and meet the other dreamers of our tribe there. The way is easy, the destination clearly marked on the map of Kandayata that all of humanity carries in its awakening memories.

As you drift into sleep at night, ask your dream-self to connect you to our people. As you are dreaming, know that you are wandering through a terrain that is shared by all human beings. So carry joy with you, carry the pride and purpose of our people, carry them with you into the collective dream realm. When you do this, you do the work of our tribe.

See yourself walking northward into the mountains. The terrain is familiar, somehow. You know where you are going. You climb higher and higher, on a path worn smooth through the years. Feel the earth beneath your feet as you climb. Smell the clear air. Notice the sun sinking behind you as you walk.

Soon, you come to the top of the mountains. Below you is a valley. In that valley is a stone-walled city. You climb down toward the city and enter its huge wooden gates just as they are about to be shut for the night. Somehow, you know this city. You head north on twisting cobbled streets, as tiny flickering lamps are lit in all the windows. Men in long indigo robes pass, nodding to you as you walk.

At the far end of the city, in the north, is a large walled temple. The walls are black and shiny. You enter through high gates and find yourself in a square stone courtyard. In the center of the courtyard is the temple itself. It is also of black stone, polished, a round domed building.

Around the temple, in each of the four directions, is a low triangular pool of water. You stop before one, remove your shoes, to wash your feet, hands, face. Having done that, beneath a starry sky, you climb the low broad steps that lead to the temple.

You push open the high narrow doors and enter the temple. It is dark within, only tiny oil lamps flickering on a raised platform in the center. Incense burns in little pots. You step in. The floors are covered in layers of white sheepskin. They are soft beneath your feet. You walk toward the center of the temple. There, rising toward the dome, carved out of a blue stone somewhat lighter in color than lapis, is an enormous cock, as tall and broad as an old oak tree.

Slowly, you move around this high stone cock, looking for a comfortable place to sleep, for this is a temple where men come together to dream. As you look around the room, you notice that there are other men, curling up on the sheepskin mats, settling into sleep. Somehow you know that all of these men are brothers in your tribe, that all of these men are fellow dreamers, that all of these men have come together for healing, for communion, in order to create in the world of day the rich and loving community that exists in our dreams.

Journey to this temple in your sleep. Ask your dream self to allow you to remember the dream within a dream you had in the temple of men. You can make this journey any night. But in the days of the ice, gay shamans came together in dream time on the night before the new moon, the night of the new moon, and the night after it. These nights are still the ideal nights for convening this way. Know too, that whoever journeys there does the work of our people. Know too that what we are creating now is new, beautiful and new. It may be rooted in the past, in the tribes of Tayarti's time, the magic of Thelki, in the shared world dreams of Kandayata. But as the branches of a tree resemble its roots, yet are not the same, what we are creating now is new, different than anything that has ever been seen on this world before. If you are sleeping alone, reach out to others in our tribe. If you are sleeping with a lover, connect your hearts as you fall into sleep. If you live in community, sleep like the spokes of a wheel, heads in the center, your hearts connected.

Sleep together, dream together, and know that you are doing the work of our people.

Never before, all over the planet, so strongly and so freely, have men who love men been able to meet in such great numbers. In this time, in our time, when spirit is more firmly rooted into matter, men who love men can come together—to hold hands, touch, sing, love, dance, speak from the heart and do the work of global healing our Divine Parents created us to do. For the rooting of spirit in matter is the work of a sentient species. And we, a scouting-people, a connecting-people, are empowered in this work by our very nature.

One of the sacred functions of the tribe of men who love men is that we are Guardians of the Trees. There is something in our nature that is like the nature of the trees themselves, for the pattern of our love creates a ladder of energy, vertical, heaven and earth connecting, just as the tree-people do. And the first thing a tree presents to you is itself, not its gender, for most trees are androgynous, bearing male and female organs together. This balance of genders is an echo of our nature. This wholeness in one body is an echo of our purpose.

Reach out to the trees. When you gather together in community, gather whenever you can in a sacred grove. As guardians of the trees, part of our work in the healing of the planet is to plant trees, join organizations that plant trees, and work to end the destruction of the planet's forests. We need to take it upon ourselves to do this work, as a community, take the lead in this time in becoming foresters, reforesters. This work with the trees is one of our sacred functions. Each time we plant another tree, we make love to

Old Man Earth again. Remember this. Remember him. Geb, Enlil, Pan, Dagda, Earth Father of a thousand long forgotten names. Remember that each tree that grows is Earth reaching out to you, with love.

In the Ice Ages, people sought comfort in their rememberings. Deep in their caves, sitting around their fires, they would tell each other stories of Lemuria, Atlantis, and Kandayata. They would take comfort in their memories, and prepare themselves for the future. They remembered the three great sacraments of Kandayata. They remembered the sacrament of woman and man loving, of those who were the guardians of the Sacred Fire, which is the sun/star of new life, the spark of the divine, the Holy Child. The image of that remembering comes to us through Isis, Osiris and Horus, through Mary, Joseph and Jesus. They also remembered the sacrament of the Sacred Well, the fountain of youth, which was guarded by women who loved women, and has come down to us in shadowed forms, in our grail myths. And they remembered the sacrament of men loving men, who were guardians of the Sacred Tree, the tree of life, the world tree. The image of this sacrament has come down to us in different places as two men standing on either side of a holy tree. Sometimes they are lovers, sometimes they are man and god, and sometimes earth god and moon god.

For so long people have thought of the moon as female, as goddess, as Ishtar, Artemis, Diana, forgetting that once the moon was seen as male, as Thoth, as Sinn. And so we look up and see the man in the moon, forgetting our own connection to him. For the Man Moon is one of the guardians of our people, this opal, changing being of the dark night sky. In legends of the old days, he was seen as the beloved of the earth, both male, both circling the mother sun together. Moon was horned god, horned just as we are, a changing god, mirroring our capacity for change. Moon stands between light and darkness, between sun and earth. And in our sacred groves, on those nights of the moon's phases, men who loved men gathered together to dance their sacred dances—just as we will dance together again.

There are many clans within a tribe, and each one has its own work to do. Some of us are more political than others, some of us more spiritual. Some of us are more male, some more female. Some of us more like the members of the main body of the tribe of all tribes, different from them only in sexual preference. Some of us are lovers of men—and of women. Some of us are in essence neither male nor female, utterly different from the people who brought us into the world. Indeed, there are worlds on which those who carry the vibration we know as gay are different in body-form from other people, just as there are worlds in which all the people are of one gender that is all genders.

There are many different clans within our tribe. In our encampments, there will be room for all of the clans, for all of the clans are needed. As we are a bridge-building people, so, too, there is a bridge within our community, one that connects the tribe of all tribes to the furthest reaches of consciousness the scouting tribes can reach. In our encampments, we must work to honor all the clans of our people, make room for all the clans of our people, and allow them to define themselves for themselves.

Sit together, walk together, sit under the moon, walk among the trees. Dance together, talk together. Find within your hearts the way to embrace each other, not exclude each other. There is no right way to be gay, no right way to be a man who loves men. All of us belong to different clans, yet each clan is needed to do the work of our tribe, each clan is needed to hold the tribe together. Scouts are not flute players, flute players are not shamans, shamans are not hunters, and hunters are not scouts. But each of us contains the energy of all the clans, in different tone, different weight, different color. Seek to find the balance within yourself, the fibers of each clan within yourself, however alien some might seem to be.

Honor the work of each clan. Know that the work of each clan is needed by the tribe of our people. Honor those who do the work you do not do. Allow their work to free you up to do your own. Honor your own work, however it seeks to express itself through you. In the great weaving of our people, every thread is needed. In the great weaving of our people, not even the greatest seers can say whose work is most sacred, most needed.

According to the Hebrew Scriptures, when the Israelites settled in the land of Canaan, the priests, the Levites were not given any tribal territory. Instead, they lived in cities scattered throughout the other tribes. So, too, will our settlements be scattered—thousands of them, everywhere across the globe, thousands of centers, encampments, for the people of our tribe to gather in. Some will be seasonal, some will be open all year. Some of us will live there all the time, others will visit from time to time. Some of us will wander like pilgrims from lodge to lodge to lodge of our people, learning, sharing, connecting. At different times in each man's life, he will turn to one of these centers, for nurturance, healing, for a communal mirror into his own sacred identity. Be he artist or healer, builder or burier, he will be welcomed by our people wherever he goes.

All of these centers will be healing spaces, sacred spaces, and yet each will have its own character. Some will be monastic retreat centers, some will become artists' colonies. Some will be schools of the healing arts, including the arts of sexual healing. There will be places for people to go on shamanic journeys, and there will also be schools for gay shamans of the next century. In some there will be children, and some will be open to women and men who seek the wisdom of our particular band of consciousness, who are not members of our own or of allied tribes.

One of our ancient roles was as midwives to the dying. Just as young men will be able to come to our encampments, so, too, will the elders of our tribe, after a life in the world, be able to come for comfort, security, to share their wisdom and be nurtured into dying, so that no man of our tribe need ever die unloved, unwanted or alone. And because of our power, some of our centers will be hospice havens for anyone in the tribe of all people to visit, there to find support in our tenderness and strength.

Many speak of rebirthing, but one of the tools of healing, in illness and in health, is to share the sacred art of re-dying. Through breath, movement and visualization, one can experience one's death, from past lives and the future. To move through death this way, to be able to release all ties and see ourselves whole and complete, is a part of the work that will be done in our encampments. This is one of the tasks of future shamans, to accompany others on the journey that all must take. In letting go, in living our dying, we become free, become fearless, make more room in our bodies for our souls to shine through, no matter what stage of life we find ourselves in.

Many of us look for healing within ourselves only. We forget that while the true healer is within, that true healing cannot happen alone. True healing happens in community, for no man's imbalance is his alone, no man's illness is his alone. Balance and imbalance are all reflections of community. Sometimes we think that healing can happen in the arms of another man. But while the eyes of flame that light the soul can always come from another's heart, true healing happens in community. We can help our lovers and be helped by them. But we cannot heal our lovers, nor can they heal us. It is only in the safety of our tribe, because of the safety of a tribe, that we are able to go inward to the deepest places, in order to be made whole, to heal ourselves.

Just as we come from every people, our power comes from what we bind together of the world. We are not a scouting people for ourselves alone. We will not go off to our retreat centers to become separate from the rest of the people. We will go off to our sacred lodges to study, heal, deepen and make ourselves ready to do our sacred work. But that work we will take back to the world, to share with the world. For our healing comes in community, our power comes from community, and our purpose comes from living in the community of the world, as healers, shamans, transformational artists.

Sometimes you look inward and cannot find the answers. But every man carries a piece of his tribesmans' answers. Through coming together, dancing, touching, praying, traveling to other realms, and speaking from the heart, each man can give what he carries to his tribal brothers, and each man can receive from his tribal brothers that which they have been carrying for him. No man is alone in this. No man carries his own information only. It is a loving act to share your healing with others. It is a piece of the past we all outgrow to think that it is only valid if we heal ourselves. Let us heal together! Heal each other! Heal in each other's hearts and hands! Make places in which to heal. This is doing the work of our sacred priesthood. This is becoming who we are.

Between lovers what is shared is the body of flesh. In community what is shared is the body of the Earth himself. Through work, through touch, through prayer, through planting and tending, in cooking and eating together, we take the holy body of the Earth into the tribal body, we bring the sacred body of the Earth into ourselves. Every plant that grows is a tree, however small, reaching out to the heavens just as we do. Remember this when you come together, for we are the guardians of the trees. Remember the sacrament of eating, that binds us to each other and to the Father who sustains us all. Thank the Earth for your food, thank the food itself for coming to you to support you in your life. Feel as you take this food inside you, that each of you takes into his body the body of the Earth. And be conscious of what you give back to the Earth, of the flesh of his body that you return to him. For we are linked to Earth in an endless cycle. Taking in, making use of, and returning. All of this is a sacrament. All of this is what binds a tribe to the Earth.

The journey to joy is the work that all of humanity is engaged in now. Joy, love, ecstasy and bliss are frequencies that permeate the universe. They are the web, the net, upon which the universe is hung. They emerge from the Prime Vibration, the Parent of all information. It is that from which all things come.

Pain and suffering have been teachers for so much of our history. Like a child who must put its hand in the fire to know what fire is, we have put our own and each other's hands in the flames, for the last ten thousand years. But just as a child learns what fire is, and how to use it rightly, so we as a species are learning how to use what can burn, to heat, to cook, to illuminate the darkness. There are worlds that have never made a journey through pain as we have. But we are coming to a time in our history when joy will be our teacher, not pain.

As difficult as it is to live with pain, it is even more difficult to live with joy. Some of us cannot imagine a world without suffering. As difficult as pain is, at least it is familiar. And joy, joy is a frequency so high, so clear, so pure, that all of the subtle fibers in our bodies must be cleansed and purified, in order to handle this frequency. No wonder it is rare, with only here and there through our history a single woman or a man being able to receive it, contain it and transmit it.

We are a people who is defined by our capacity for love. So who amongst all people, if not us, should be in the vanguard of Earth folk who are making the journey to joy? To let joy in, we must be cleansed in all our fibers, must be virgins again. Then, we can work to open our bodies to the universal frequency that is Mother Sky, and ground it in our bodies by becoming one with Earth Father. To do this is the holiest work of our priesthood.

This cannot happen overnight. This cannot be done alone. In this place, in this time, no individual is strong enough to channel in this energy alone. Two together loving can cleanse each other's fibers, rewire each other on increasingly more subtle frequencies. Yes, lovers can do this with each other. But it is only in community, that any two, or any one, can be so firmly grounded, so centered, so connected, that joy can flow freely in, and flow freely out again. Together we create one vast and open body of men that is able to draw in, hold, ground and beam out joy to the world. In this is our priesthood, in this our destiny, to become, each one of us, another column in the living temple of Heaven on Earth.

A cycle of human history is coming to an end. What began ten thousand years ago comes to its completion, and a new cycle of history begins, another ten thousand years. Just as there are trees like yews, sequoias and bristlecone pines that live for thousands of years, hardy and enduring, so too have we endured as a people, nameless, homeless, disconnected from our kin. In secret, whispered by lover to lover, in silence, in the collective memory of our species, down through these long years our nature and purpose have remained alive. Some of us have carried it in and out of bodies. Others of us have stepped into it for the first time. But it lives, our ancient/future history. And now we reclaim it for ourselves, our tribal heirs, and for all of humanity.

It is in triumph, in beauty and in power that we and all the other scouting peoples find each other, remember our powers, create new encampments, and take our rightful places in the tribe of all tribes. For we enter a new era in our history. We enter an era when love and not pain will be our teacher, when joy and not sorrow will color our lives. Never before on this planet have people lived this way. But after thousands and thousands of years of struggle and growth, we have come to the point in time when all of us will be fully incarnate in our bodies, fully present as spirits manifesting in physical form. Without our wisdom and our power, humanity cannot make it to the next cycle. With our power and our wisdom, shared freely with the tribe of all tribes, everything is possible.

Let us bless the tribe of all tribes that brought us into the world, bless the people through whose sacred bodies other people come. Let us bless all the scouting peoples, whose ancient and long forgotten wisdom is being remembered in this time. And let us bless each other and ourselves. It is for this that our ancestors worked, that we ourselves worked in other lives—so that all of humanity, and we the tribe of men who love men, can step into this new era, the time of love on Earth.

Part Four:
The Awakening
of the Joy-Body

Joy Is a Frequency
That Permeates the Universe

From small towns and suburbs, from cities and farms, alone and with others, we are coming together again. From shame and with pride, in love and with sorrow, from fear and with hope, we are coming together again as a tribe, as a people. And in this time we enter the fifth era of our history. Our history is long, however forgotten it has been. Our history is rich, however outcast we have been. Our history is glorious, and we are coming to reclaim it. Our history is nurturing. To know it roots us in the world.

In the days of Tayarti we came together as a people. That was the first era of our history. We built our temples in the second era. As the patriarchy spread and we began to lose our power, we entered the third era. And when the priests of monotheism railed against us, we went underground to survive era four. But the world has changed. From Ice Age to Atom Age, from one kind of death to another we have survived. We have moved around the circle of time, from East to South to West to North. And now we come back to East and to the beginning again. To a time of rebirth and renewal. To a time of purpose and destiny. A time to remember our history. A time to awaken our bodies to joy.

In the days of Tayarti, people lived in joy. They lived fully awake as their bodies. In our evolution as a species we have moved away from joy. In exploring our minds and the world we have divided, dissected, defined, and destroyed. But we are coming back to wholeness again, to Oneness, and to joy. Down through the dark ages of our history, it has been love that allowed us to survive. And in the next era of our history, it will be joy that heals us and renews us as a people.

Feel the flickering of joy in your heart. Feel the shimmering of joy in your body. Feel joy in the earth and the sky. Breathe in joy and breathe it out again. Joy is a frequency that permeates the universe. Joy is the breath of the Divine.

The Clans of Our History

The world at the end of the last Ice Age, the world of Tayarti and his followers, was very different from the world we live in, and very different from the world of present day "Stone Age" peoples. Gender and sex roles were fluid. Family structures were fluid. At that time the great tribe of all the people was divided up into 24 different patterns of movement in the world, 24 different clans, in four major groups. These clans covered all of human experience, and right beneath the surface of our conscious minds—they continue to do so to this day. Below you will find each clan and the image that identifies it.

Organizational, aggressive, day focused, often male:

Elder		Warrior	
Chief		Scout	
Hunter		Trader	

Creative, transformational, night-focused:

Dancer		Storyteller	
Drummer		Fire Keeper	
Flute Player		Shaman	

Nurturing and providing figures, often female:

Midwife		Shelter Maker	
Tender of the Young		Food Maker	
Water Carrier		Seed Carrier	

Craftspeople:

Potter		Garment Maker	
Weaver		Tool Maker	
Basket Maker		Maker of Images	

If you look through this list you will get a sense of what life was like 10,000 years ago, get a picture of what people did, how they moved through the world. Now look through the list of clans again—but this time, look at each clan as an archetypal pattern imprinted onto all of human consciousness. Take all the occupations of our time and connect them back to their roots. An architect would be a Shelter Maker, a third grade teacher would be a Tender of the Young, your friend who does silk screen T-shirts would be a Maker of Images, an electrical engineer might be a Fire Keeper, your psychotherapist is a Shaman, the woman who does consulting work for your boss is a Seed Carrier, a drag queen up all night sewing is a Garment Maker. That Internet wiz you know is a Weaver, a Scout. And whenever you sit down at a computer, you are a Storyteller and a Basket Maker, creating soft containers to hold information in. Which clans do you belong to? Which energies do you work with?

These 24 clans exist in human consciousness just as solidly as Stonehenge exists in the world. They are one way of talking about purpose. In this time of human history, all of us participate in many different clans. Explore the ones that you belong to. And as a people in this era, we include many clans, too. The ancient four-fold tribal image of who we are as Scouts, Flute Players, Shamans, and Hunters will always be the skeleton of our nature. But in between those four watch-points, every other clan is woven in. Feel in yourself and in our people the weaving together of these ancient, archytypal clans. Breathe them in and feel their aliveness in all of your cells. Drink up the clans of our history through your roots, just as a tree drinks up water from the earth. And bask in the radiant joy that shines in your cells as you drink this liquid in. For the past is alive in us. And from it, we create ourselves anew.

How To Begin To Become Everything

Tayarti was born about 12,000 years ago, in a tiny encampment at the foot of the Pyrenees in what is now France. He taught his students many things, from dance to working with herbs. Every morning he had his students do the following exercise, to expand their awareness of what it means to be human, a man who loves men, a consciousness shifter, and to expand their ability to be a container for joy. Practicing this exercise will expand your personhood, and doing this with a partner will exercise the subtle fibers of your energy bodies and support you in aligning with each other.

This exercise is a combination of physical postures and meditation. You do it sitting on the ground with one leg crossed over the other, not in lotus position. It doesn't matter which leg is on top. The exercise has four sections, each of which is separated by what I call a lock. To do the lock, drop your head to your chest, put your tongue on the roof of your mouth, suck in your breath, contract your anal sphincter for a quick count of seven, to hold the pattern in your body and lock it in. The purpose of the exercise is to teach you to become everything, from a stone to the sun. When you assume each position, do not just feel it physically, but allow yourself to become it. Leave human consciousness behind. Become a stone. Be dense, inert, and allow yourself to experience rock consciousness, stone consciousness. Go through each step and *become* it. Use each step as a journey through consciousness. And at the end of each segment, feel and hold the information in your body of what it means to be those four different kinds of Being.

Know when you are doing this exercise that you are not just learning to become all things, but you are also connecting with tribes of men who loved men who did this work thousands of years ago. In connecting with them, we honor them, our ancestors, and learn to stand proudly in the world again as they did.

The meditations in each step are as follows:

Section one:

STONE begins when you bring your knees up toward your chest, with your legs crossed in front of you. Wrap your arms around your legs, drop your head between your knees, and become a stone.

To do TREE, lower your legs to the original position, crossed. Then raise your arms toward the sky, spread out like branches. Turn your face to the sky.

For MOUNTAIN, your legs remain the same. Place your hands on the ground on either side of you, fingers pointing away from your body, so that your head and arms and hands make a triangle.

In STREAM, your legs are still the same. Place one hand in front of your body, palm flat on the ground, in front of where your legs cross. Place your other hand behind you, palm up, near your sacrum. Feel a current washing through you, from hand to hand. Then do the lock that completes this first segment.

Section two:

To do CLOUD, sit with your legs crossed (for this and for all remaining positions). Your arms are to the side at shoulder level, elbows bent, with one hand up and one hand down. The palm of the higher hand faces up, the palm of the lower hand faces down. Switch hands until you find the position that feels most fluid and insubstantial to you.

For WIND, bring your arms in front of your chest. Cup your hands one on top of the other, palms facing each other, about six inches apart. Feel a spiral of energy moving through your body. Become wind.

In LIGHTNING, point one arm up toward the sky at an angle. Point the other one down so that your arms create an oblique line through your body. Become charged, electric.

For THUNDER, bring your hands in front of your chest. Make fists and hold one above the other, clenched tightly, a few inches apart, about to pound together. Do not pound them, but rather feel the energy gathering in you that is thunder. Then do the lock again.

Section three:

MOON - Put one hand on top of your head, the other on your navel. Feel this crescent. Feel yourself glowing silver.

SUN - Place both hands on top of your head. Be fiery, radiant, golden, vast.

EARTH - place both hands on your navel. Be round, alive, be our world.

SEA - arms to your side at shoulder level, elbows bent up, fingers pointing up, so that hands and arms assume a wave shape, become ocean. Feel it surging through you until you are it. Now spread beyond it and become the cosmic sea. Then do the lock.

Section four:

DEER - put your hands on top of your head facing forward, with your fingers pointing up and spread out like antlers, your mind and body alert, poised to leap through the trees.

BEAR - put your hands on the ground in front of you, with your knuckles curled. Put your weight on your knuckles and your knees, and raise your sacrum off the ground a little bit, as if you were lumbering through the forest.

EAGLE - extend your arms behind you, palms facing each other about four inches apart. These are your wings. Now lean forward, look down, and feel yourself soaring over the earth.

TURTLE - drop your face almost all the way to the ground. Palms on the ground, put your hands near your hips, fingers pointing behind you.

End by coming back to a regular sitting position, hands in your lap, for the final lock. And as you look around you and move in the world, what do you see that you want to become, that you can add to your practice? Dog, snail, chair, oven, typewriter, blanket, refrigerator—there is no end to what you can become. Use this as a daily spritual practice. You will notice that you move in the world differently when everything you move with and through and under and over is something that you can become.

One of the lies we have been telling ourselves is that the Creator is separate from Creation, and we are separate from everything around us. In truth, there is no separation, except in our thoughts. The Earth is not flat, in spite of appearances, and we are not separate, even when we feel that we are. The more you do this exercise, the more you will feel, begin to become, and participate in the Oneness of all of life. Then you too will be a living container for joy.

Healing Your Wounds
and Owning Your Power

A shadow is a wound cast outward. A wound is a shadow turned in. In our journey toward joy we need to work with both of them, with our personal wounds and shadows, and with our collective injuries as well.

By nature we are a compassionate and non-judgmental people. But our historical oppression has separated us from our true power. Boxed in and hated, we have absorbed the cultural hatred around us, and bounced it back and forth between ourselves. Sometimes, this internalized hatred has been transformed into camp, into high humor. But often it has been turned into bitchiness or verbal attack, the only form of anger or male power allowed us. Recognize this, acknowledge that we do it, then turn inward to your five-chambered heart, and step out into the world from a place of compassion again.

Part of our strength is our fluidity, our capacity to change, to disguise ourselves on stages self-created and otherwise, to pass for things that we are not, to be invisible. But there is another side to this strength. We can be liars, we can get trapped in deception, social and romantic. We can waste our lives pretending to be things that we are not. We can be superficial, obsessed with image and attitude. Now, honor your capacity for invention, for dreaming, for fantasy, and come back to your innate fluidity again. Sing from it, dance from it, cook from it, move from it, laugh from it, sleep from it. Own your genius, own your splendor.

One of our powers is that we are able to walk between the genders. But often this becomes polarized, and we can get locked into one or the other. How often have we been passive, indecisive, vague, afraid to express our opinions or to own our power? Told we were not real men, we have been female caricatures, fickle, flighty, waiting for others to make decisions for us. Or in reclaiming our maleness, we have gotten trapped into cold, arrogant, body-armored disconnection, vanity, contempt that pretends to be achievement. But feel your male and femaleness together. Know that you are not one, not the other, but both and more. You are a member of the Walks-Between People. Honor everyone you walk past with this knowing.

As consciousness scouts we have been disenfranchised by our society, marginal people. If we meet at all it is in the confines of a ghetto, not woven into the world. The dominant culture has tried to lock all outside peoples into patterns of dependence, poverty, drugs, alcohol, shattered families, in order to keep us powerless. By defining us in restrictive ways, we are prevented from taking control of our lives and using them to heal and transform our communities, and to take our place in the community of all peoples. So reclaim your power as a scouting person. Honor all the ways that you scout for yourself, our tribe, and for all tribes. The world as we know it would stop if we all took back our scouting talents. Stand proudly now, and celebrate all of our gifts.

As shamans, we may flourish in the healing arts, or lose all connection to the soul work that led us to become hair dressers, decorators, nurses. The further we have moved from our powers, the more wounded we have become. But beneath our wounds is power. Feel that power. All of our addictions, to chemicals and to behaviors, mask our ancient shaman powers. Honor these wounds, thank them for teaching us and thank them for bringing us to where we are now. And release them, in any and every way you know how. Take into yourself only nurturing substances, and give back to the world your healers gifts.

We are midwives for the dying, yet we have often turned that gift inside out, taking our own lives, quickly, or slowly through our addictions. And we are creators of beauty. Yet so often we create beauty for others, and surround ourselves with ugliness, feeling unworthy. In the ancient days the temple priests understood that beauty is a part of healing. We who have been known as beauty makers have remembered this in a partial way. Now it is time for us to work with beauty again, to make it and be it and use it in our work. The healing of the planet depends upon our honoring beauty, which is not about how something *looks* but rather about how it *feels*, about its integrity, its capacity to be in harmony with everything around it. So honor the beauty of the planet. Create beauty in and around you, in everything you do, from the spaces you work in and the music you play to the words and touch and thoughts and inner feelings that you carry.

Our sexuality has been hidden for so long, denied for so long, lied about for so long. And yet it is also the way that we have celebrated our being alive, and shared in a deep and wordless brotherhood. Not allowed to act in the world, so much of our physicality has been channeled into sex, until it became an obsession. We use each other for sex, use sex to fulfill other needs, reject each other because of sex, use it as a bargaining tool, a toy for our egos, and forget that we were put on this earth to make love. We forget love in our hunger for flesh, we forget our own and our brothers' capacity for love. We fear love, much as we hunger for it.

There are also deep, unconscious sexual wounds that we carry as a community. In the past, in cultures across the planet, men of our people were castrated. In some places this was done for ritual reasons, and in others for political ones. In some places we were seen as outcasts, and in others, now crippled, we were allowed to be priests, bureaucrats, with limited power.

There were also places on this planet where men of our people were safe only when they had renounced sex. Often these men were members of various priesthoods, and often they lived their lives in isolation, in pain. Because we are all connected to our tribe's collective unconscious, these patterns touch all men who love men. Sensing these old wounded places, some of us have plunged into our sexuality, attempting to reclaim the use of lost genitals and lost sexuality. And some of us have isolated ourselves, feeling inadequate, undeserving of love or sexual expression, without knowing the depths of these feelings. We have been sexual victims of other men's rage at us. And for many of us, our secret sexual lives have taken place beside deconstructed trees, by streams, that are stalls and public toilets, the last reflection of our once having been the guardians of the trees.

Put your hands on your genitals. Deepen into yourself and feel that all of us carry the memory of sacrificed testicals and penis, and that many men still experience, in early infancy, genital mutilation. Feel the sorrow there, the pain, the shame, the fear. Feel the ways that all of us have sacrificed the integrity of our bodies, the wholeness of our love and capacity for touch. And breathe now. Feel now waves of golden light that come to you from our tribe, from our people past, present, future. Breathe in this golden light and let in heal these wounds.

With yourself, with friends, partners, others, look at our wounds and shadows, and see them with compassion. When any one of us does this, it shifts the energy that surrounds our tribe. When all of us do this we will have created a web of energy around our tribe that will be safe and strong, whole and healed, alive and beautiful. For a luminous body casts no shadow around itself.

Once children were born into a world where sex and pleasure and love were honored. To create a world like that again we must remove the fears, the shame, the lies we have been telling ourselves—that the world is not real, not valid, that only spirit is real and valid. It is time for us to honor the world of physicality, the world of the senses. For it is real, it is holy, and as beings who chose to enter physicality, our destiny can only be fulfilled here.

As a daily meditation, imagine a world where everyone is conceived in love and pleasure, delivered in love and pleasure, where there is no fear or shame of any physical processes. Imagine a world where everyone is awakened to desire and love, in joy and celebration, where there is no loneliness, no hunger, no desperation, where no one ever uses anyone else for sex, because sex always emerges from love, and the nature of love is understood by everyone as part of the prime vibration, the ground of all being.

Love is the key here, for the second lie that we as a people have been told is that men who love men are incapable of love. But in the future world we are creating, all forms of love will be celebrated, and men will meet each other in joy and celebration, not in fear, anger or shame.

Sex in a world of love is a physical act, and a sacred one. It is a recreational activity *and* a sacrament. It is not about exchanging bodily fluids, but about exchanging soul information with another man on the deepest and most intimate level. As a sacrament, it is joyous, fun, and deeply pleasurable. To believe anything else is the third lie we must heal ourselves of, that spirituality has to be serious. In a world where everyone celebrates their bodies and all of creation, sacredness is sensuous, sublime, splendid, seductively silly.

Tasting Joy in Your Body

There is a primal force, the Creator of all that is. Whether we call it God or Goddess, it is the same Oneness. From the heart of this Oneness, four forces flow that sustain the universe. Physicists call them gravity, electromagnetism, the strong force, and the weak force. I call them love, joy, ecstasy, and bliss. We human beings are a weaving together of these four forces. The work of the past, the work of the spiritual teachers of the past, has been about love. But as we evolve it is time for us to explore who we are as beings of joy.

Joy is the name for the single energy that we have seen as two distinct ones, as spiritual energy and sexual energy. The sharing of joy will be the major healing tool of the future. Dolphins and whales understand this, that free-flowing joy is the balance to love, the cross-weave in the fabric of life, able to hold all our pain and sorrow in its embrace.

We have been disconnected from joy for so long that it takes time for us to feel it in our bodies. The best technique I know for awakening joy is this. Each morning when you get up, touch yourself all over, massage yourself from head to toe. Joy is everywhere, and we have all been raised in a culture of fear and contraction. As you touch yourself, as you relax, speak softly to your skin, your muscles, your organs, your bones, your cells. As you massage yourself, say aloud to every part you touch, "This finger is holy. This elbow is sacred. These ribs are blessed. This stomach is sacred. This shin bone is holy. These balls, this cock, this asshole are blessed." Say this out loud to every part of you, inner and outer. Touch every part of you, inside your ears and mouth, up into your armpits and under your balls. In blessing and naming every part of yourself, you will heal the separation between soul and body. Then joy will flow easily, in and out of every cell.

Afterwards, you may want to pleasure yourself, to raise erotic energy. When this energy is strong, breathe it up into your abdomen and your chest, into your heart. Fill your heart with this energy. Feel it pulsing in your arteries and veins. If there is any part of your physical body that is tense, in pain, in need of healing, breathe this energy into that part. Use it to heal yourself. Breathe this energy into your hands. Feel it pouring out of your palms and your fingertips. Touch yourself with this energy, fill yourself with it, heal and bless yourself with it. Let the path grow familiar and strong from cock to heart to hands.

If there are places in your neighborhood or anywhere on the planet that are troubled and in need of healing, beam the energy that fills your body out to them, from your heart, your hands or wherever feels right to you. Fill the airwaves with pleasure. Beam it out everywhere. Pleasure yourself and send this energy out into the heavens and down into the earth. Make love to everything this way, to clouds and rocks and planets and stars.

Beam this energy into your food before you eat. This will both energize it and tune it to your body so that you can digest it fully and efficiently. If you are taking herbs or medications, beam it into them too, to tune them to your body the same way.

When you connect with someone, remember that he is far more than just a physical body. Even when you are talking on the phone, he is touching you and you are touching him. The moment he walks in the door, even if you are 20 feet away, your subtle body is touching him and his subtle body is touching you. What do you feel? What do you see? Pay attention to all of this before you touch hands.

When you are with someone, sense all the layers of his body. See how the energy flows in his body. Where does it flow smoothly and where does it get stuck? This is part of what our ancestors knew how to do. Subtle touch, the touch of energy before the touch of hands, is a part of love-making, too. Remember that you can overload someone's circuits, give too much energy, or give it too quickly.

A lover of men must know how to be intimate. Intimacy is a state in which energy flows freely from person to person, in and out of every organ, in and out of every cell. But many people are filled with love and still unhappy, because they do not know how to transmit it to others, or do not know how to receive it. Is your heart open? Can you give and receive love equally well? Can you give and receive love equally well—at the same time?

Go back over your personal history. Explore all your relationships, with family, friends, and lovers. Where was there intimacy and where was there need? Where was there intimacy and where was there fear?

If you are having difficulty being intimate, sit with a beautiful flower. Beam out energy from your heart to the flower, until it is filled with it. Then feel how the flower is beaming energy back to you with no reservations. Breathe in this joyous energy and be filled with it, in every part of you. When you are able to be intimate with flowers, go on to trees, to animals and then on to humans. To be able to do this, to be heart-centered, is what we came here for. Feel your heart spread out until it fills your entire body. Beam the energy of your heart out to the world, and let the world send it back to you.

Two Men Together

In ancient times, everyone knew that the love two people shared was not shared for themselves alone, but for and with the entire community. Shared love became a conduit for higher energies entering the physical plane. Sometimes this was seen as a sacred marriage, be it between a man and a woman, two women or two men. Through their union, two were known to be able to draw in archetypal energy, to anchor it in form.

The archetypal patterns of A Man and A Woman Together, Two Women Together, and Two Men Together were laid down in the collective unconscious long before there was a sense of goddesses and gods, in the time before the ice, when people still encountered Oneness directly. To be whole, a culture needs to cultivate each of the three primary love patterns, for each carries a different energy. Two women together create a storage vessel for the collective. Two men together broadcast out that information to the collective. A man and a woman together celebrate the doorway to embodiment through their being together.

As we journey into the future, we must also spiral back to the foundations of human consciousness to find our roots, so that we can build on them anew. The patterns in the collective unconscious are like mountain ranges, changing slowly, that define for us the horizon against which we see Eternity.

Only vestiges of this understanding remain in our culture, and only in the union of a woman and a man. The wedding ceremony has lost its deeper energetic functions, and only the outer form has survived. The wedding cake is all that remains of the sacred hill the lovers met on. The figures on top of the cake are all that remain of the god and goddess the two would embody. The eating of the cake is the last vestige of the communal sharing of energy that sealed the couples' union in the heart of their community. For a true marriage binds together heaven and the earthly community. The drawing in of the archetypal energies, however unconscious, helped to anchor a couple in their union. But now, not even heterosexual unions work, and we move further and further from any sense of purpose.

In ancient times, two women or two men coming together had their own different rituals, and they are even more forgotten than heterosexual rituals. We have forgotten the passing of the great water goblet that recalled our fluidness, the fire that symbolized our passion, the stone that was Father

Earth, the feather that was Mother Sky, bound to the wooden staff that was the sign of our people, given to the two who were bonded, as a symbol of their union. But it is time for us to remember what once was, what lives on still in the collective unconscious. In remembering, in coming back to the roots of how two men come together, we resanctify our love and make it holy for ourselves and for everyone in our community. As more and more of us do this, the world will see us again in our sacredness, and honor us again for our purpose in the greater scheme of human life.

Two men together are able through their love to embody the energetic patterns established by the earliest men who loved men. In drawing in the archetypal energy, three things occur. The lovers experience deeper and more creative intimacy, the energies of heaven and earth are woven together in yet another place, and this energy is beamed out to everyone through their bodies, blessing all and feeding all.

In the Temple of Your Daily Life

When we embody the archetype Two Men Together, we awaken an innate holiness. The following exercises are designed to deepen the connection between two lovers, so that your priesthood can be grounded, balanced and expansive at the same time.

Except for the first and last, the exercises that follow are to be done sitting face to face. Unless it is indicated, you may sit on the floor, cross-legged, or in chairs, with your feet on the floor. Sitting is a middle position, between standing and lying down. This middle position facilitates the work.

These exercises make shifts in the energetic structures of both partners. Old blockages, shadows, and wounds, will come to the surface—physically, mentally and emotionally. Release whatever comes up by using your breath to clear the old patterns out of your body and mind. This may be a very slow process, as new layers rise to the surface. Be gentle and compassionate with each other's limits and boundaries, remembering how long you have carried these wounds, remembering that some of them are deeply locked into our tribal memory. Honor yourself and seek help if you need it. You don't have to do this alone.

These exercises create shifts. As you go through them, more does not equal better. Do each exercise:

1) only once a week

2) in a safe and quiet place where you know that you will not be interrupted

3) for about five, and no more than ten, minutes at a time, unless the exercise instructs you to do otherwise

4) do not go on to the next exercise until you are comfortable with the one you have been working on

Bonding Exercise Number One

Stand facing each other, without clothes on. Be aware of your breathing, and match your breath to your partner's.

Slowly, one of you approach the other, and touching every part of your lover's body, say these words right into his skin: "Your stomach is holy. Your ribs are holy. Your spine is holy." Work from toes to head, naming every part, inner and outer. End by holding him and whispering in his ear, "All of your cells are holy. You are holy, you are blessed, you are sacred."

Switch, and now the one who touched will be touched.

After doing this a few times, bless each other's bodies at the same time, so that your words weave together. You may also want to try it lying down.

Bonding Exercise Number Two

Sit face to face. Be conscious of your breath. Synchronize your breathing.

Look into each other's eyes.

As if your eyes were headlights, one of you beam energy into the other's eyes, so that he can take it in.

Switch partners, so that receiver is now the energy sender.

When each of you are comfortable sending and taking in, let the energy flow in both directions at the same time.

Bonding Exercise Number Three

Sit facing each other, synchronize your breathing as you gaze into each other's eyes.

Partner one, beam out love from your heart to your partner's heart.

Partner two, open your heart and allow yourself to receive the love your partner beams toward you.

When you are comfortable doing this, switch so that the sender becomes the receiver, and the receiver becomes the sender.

Give yourselves as long as you want to do this. When you are comfortable sending and receiving love separately, play with each of you sending love out of your hearts and also receiving it, so that you can connect your hearts at the same time.

Bonding Exercise Number Four

Sitting, facing each other, synchronize your breathing.

Look into each other's eyes.

Connect your hearts.

Bring your hands up so that your palms are facing each other, about a foot apart, feeling that the energetic connection between them is the same that you exchanged when you touched each other in the first exercise.

Tone together, any way you want to. Continue to breathe, making eye contact.

Do this for five minutes at first. Then, gradually, increase your time until you can do this for ten minutes.

Bonding Exercise Number Five

Sit in chairs, your knees a foot apart. Synchronize your breathing.

Make eye contact.

Connect your hearts.

Now, breathe in heaven energy through the top of your head, and exhale it into the earth, through the bottoms of your feet.

Breathe up earth energy through your feet, and send it up into the heavens through the top of your head.

Hold your palms a foot apart and feel the energy that passes between them.

Tone together, and do this for as long as feels comfortable to you, for up to twenty minutes.

Bonding Exercise Number Six

Sit, facing each other and synchronize your breathing.

Connect eyes.

Connect your hearts.

Breathe in and out heaven and earth energy.

Lightly hold each other's cocks in your hands, experimenting to see what position works best for you. You do not have to be aroused. When you find a comfortable position, simply hold each other.

Instead of toning out loud, feel the vibration of the energy flowing in and between you, and be with the silent sound.

Do this for up to twenty minutes, breathing together.

Bonding Exercise Number Seven

In the sitting position, synchronize your breathing.

Connect eyes.

Connect hearts.

Breathe in and out heaven and earth energy.

Hold each other's cocks.

Feel the vibration passing between you.

Feel and see yourselves sitting in the midst of a vast column of radiant light that rises far up into the heavens and far down into the earth, circling around you both about two feet behind your backs.

This column of light is the essence of the archetype, Two Men Together. Feel it washing in and out of your body, a luminous vertical ocean, washing all around you, into your bodies, into your hearts. Hold it in your hearts.

Know and feel that you are connected in this energy to all the men who have loved men since the beginning of time.

Know and feel that you are shining your light out to all the men who will love men, in the world today, and in the future, blessing all of them.

Know that the love you share is a blessing for all of humanity, for the earth, and for all of creation.

Bask in your radiant shared energy. Feel it beaming out and in, illuminating the world. Feeling this, breathe together, be together and let this light carry you back into the room, your lives, and carry this light back with you.

Bonding Exercise Number Eight

When you are comfortable with the forms of the first seven bonding exercises, let go of them. Be loving together. Know that you are the embodiment in the present of the ancient archetype Two Men Together.

Do anything you feel like doing together. Walk, talk, be silent. Dance, cook, make love.

Know that whatever you do together is sacred, holy, blessed. For so long our bodies have been asleep. But now we awaken them, we awaken them to joy, we awaken them to the power of our tribe again.

Places To Go When You Come

For many of us orgasm is the goal of sex, the end, the reason to have it. It is important to remember that an orgasm is a microcosm in our bodies of the same energy that created the physical universe. In other words, when the Creator came, the Big Bang occurred, and our universe came into being. Whenever we have an orgasm, we tap into that same energy and experience it all over again. Our ancient elders knew this, that each orgasm is a mini Big Bang, a moment of Nothingness, not the end of a process but a journey of manifestation back into light and form again, a holy new beginning.

In the first moments after an orgasm, a man is able to encounter his soul directly, and swim in the realm of pure eternal bliss. In this state of consciousness a man can experience the spark of the Divine that has created him, meet the god who is himself. Doing this is a rebirth and a blessing, not just for him but for all of life, and is the first of three post-orgasmic states.

To do this, you and your partner should create a quiet time when you know you will not be interrupted. Make yourselves comfortable. You may want to sit with your partner cradled in your lap and bring him to orgasm with your hand. There is a physical support you can use to guide your partner into the first post-orgasmic state. At the time of ejaculation, breathe with your partner, and cup the fingers of your other hand on his occipital protruberance, the bump on the back of the skull right above the neck. Gently rock it with the smallest of motions, turning it in small circles from side to side. Doing this will will support his entry into the state of post-orgasmic consciousness where he may become aware of his soul.

The second level of post-orgasmic consciousness can take a man back to before his birth. Being in that state will allow him to reconnect with other lives and with why he chose to be born now, and what he came here to explore, experience and accomplish. Knowing this can be healing and useful in the journey to life transformation. Entry into the second post-orgasmic state may begin as his breathing begins to slow down, but just before he would normally become conscious of his surroundings again. It can be facilitated by slipping your hand down your lover's neck so that your fingers are resting on the seventh cervical vertebra, the prominent one at the base of his neck. Cup your fingertips around it and gently rock it slowly from left to right and back again, lightly, softly, over and over.

In the third level, he can remember his own conception, and flow out from that moment all through his life until he comes back to the present, back to the light. By going there, he will be able to see all his gifts, and see also the wounds, blockages and healing he needs to do to come back to a state of wholeness again. So ushering your beloved into that place is a wonderful gift to give him.

The shift from state two to three begins as his heartbeat begins to return to normal. To guide entry into the third post-orgasmic state, slide your hand around the front of your companion's body. Place your thumb and fingertips lightly over his sternum and his second set of ribs. They are easy to find, just about an inch below the notch of the clavicle, jutting out. Hold this area in your fingertips and gently rock it up and down with the breath so that your fingers are just slightly exaggerating the up-and-down motion of the rib cage with each inhalation and exhalation.

How do you carry each other into these states? How do you go there yourself? First, you need to know that these places exist. Second, you have to create an atmosphere of safety and expansion that will not force you to jump right back into your skin, but one that will encourage you to step out of time, or at least let time slow down enough so that you can shift your awareness. When you do this, you also have to know that you will in time come back to your normal, waking consciousness again.

Darkness is helpful in this journey. Because we are afraid of the darkness, because we are disconnected from soul-sense, the moment an orgasm is over, we leap back into our bodies, back into our usual consciousness, or fall right to sleep, missing this wonderful journey. But when we come to know and trust the darkness, it will nurture us in return.

On this journey, music is not recommended. We need to drift in our own rhythms. Feel your partner's rhythm as you hold him and whisper it back to him with your breath, rock him and help him to deepen into it.

The first time you go on this journey, it may be a quick one. But gradually, you will learn to stretch out the moment of darkness after orgasm, so that you can stay in and explore each of the three post-orgasmic states for longer and longer periods of time, or rather, no-time.

This work is a personal vision quest, deep into the nature of one's own being. It is a journey into timelessness, to the soul manifesting itself in form. This is not a journey to go on every day. A good time to share this with your lover is on the night of the new moon. The map of the journey is in our collective unconscious, laid down by generations of ancestors who went there. And when we tap into the pattern of Two Men Together, when we are in a place of trust and tenderness, it is easy to go there.

Meeting Our Tribal Ancestors

The universe is a pulsing network of information, flowing endlessly from place to place. Within this network are countless different frequencies, linking together everything from sub-atomic particles to entire galaxies. Each world carries its own set of frequencies, ranging from the vast to the microscopic. For example, all the world's viruses are connected in an energetic web, and each particular kind of virus is joined by its own sub-frequency.

In the same way, all of humanity is linked together in a single information frequency that surrounds and permeates this planet. Within this larger frequency there are numerous smaller information bands that link together members of each race, each gender, each faith, each tribe, each vocation, etc. And among the thousands of discrete frequencies that pulse within the greater human frequency, we find that of the tribe of men who love men.

Just as radio waves and television waves permeate a room, invisible and yet present, all of these frequencies permeate the globe. Little boys who have chosen to love others of their own gender, who grow up in small towns in the middle of nowhere, with no role models, with no one to tell them about themselves, are just as plugged into their chosen tribal frequency as are boys growing up in the largest of cities, with gay uncles and cousins and friends. We are never alone.

Most of us never become conscious of the vast amounts of information that we are plugged into. We live our lives in isolation from each other and from the rich history of our people that is carried in our shared man-loving frequency. From the beginning of human time on this world, any man who loved another man was tied into this frequency, and all of our history was thus recorded, preserved, and is available when we are ready to make it conscious.

You are always in unconscious contact with the ancestors who carry all this information, here, in Thelki and in other realms. You may encounter them in post-orgasmic states. And Two Men Together may want to tap in more consciously to the wisdom of our people, and the following process will suport you if you and your parter want to do this.

Sit together face to face, and do Bonding Exercise Number Seven. While you are sitting in the midst of your column of light, feel that sitting in a circle around you are the ancestors of our people. Like a stone tossed into a pond, you and your partner are rippling outward. Feel this ripple, and expand your minds and energy bodies to include it. Feel, sense, see, listen. Like fishermen, cast out strands of your mind into the waters of gay consciousness. If you have questions about who you are and who we are as a people, cast them out into the waves. Invoke the ancestors from each of the four gay clans, those of the East, South, West, and North, going around the circle in this way to call them in. Like reference librarians in a vast fluid library of gay consciousness, these men who love men, disembodied, who have chosen to hold this information and share it with us, will be there to meet you.

Another wonderful way to open to the ancestors is to do the bonding exercise in bed just before you fall asleep. Dream is the doorway for ancestors, angels, the Divine, to weave themselves into our thoughts and communicate with us. With another or alone, open yourself and invite the ancestors in. As you drift into sleep, place your hands on your heart and call out to them.

The words of this book have come to me in just this way. The stories, visions and dreams of this book have come to you through me from our ancestors, in this and other worlds in just this way. Alone, or as anchors and grounding for each other, you and your lover can participate in our lost history, and discover, as I have, that nothing is lost, that thousands of years of man-loving are alive in the energetic airwaves of our planet.

The Angel of Our People

Every relationship, every family, every office, school, and each clan, tribe, nation, community has its own shared information field. Within each field we will encounter its rooting ancestors. And each field has an overseer, a connecting angel, who holds within its body all the individual members, and all the collective history of that group.

Since the days when humankind first appeared on this world, an angel named Altus has been the connecting angel for the tribe of men who love men. It was assigned this task by the high angels who oversee the growth and development of the human species on this planet, along with hosts of other angels who were assigned to other different communities.

In Altus' living body is all of our history. Its living body contains the lives and deeds and hopes and visions of every man who has loved another man, deeply and from the essence of his being in a given incarnation. It is through Altus that we can reach out to Thelki and other gay realities. Whenever a man on our planet has activated the inner subtle fibers that allow him to love another man, that energy has resonated him into Altus' body.

Altus is the vessel that contains us all, just as other vessels contain deaf people, Muslims, potters, auto mechanics and, ultimately, all human beings.

Sit together in a column of light. Expand your consciousness outward to the furthest limits of that light and feel Altus' body. Call on Altus. Feel its ancient presence, know that it is through Altus that however alone you felt in your childhood and youth, you survived because some part of you knew that you had your own family, your own people. And with this inner knowing that comes from being connected to Altus, you did what you had to to find yourself, to find our people, to find love. For some peoples are bound together by a shared love or land, others by mutual history, common ancestors, or shared beliefs. But we are a people that is bound together by the capacity to love. And when we lost our shared history, lost our sense of place in the world, still we found each other. We found each other because Altus, a being of love, has always connected us in its love. Love grounds and sustains us in the world, in our manhood, our creativity. Love shines in the center of our five-chambered hearts. Love flows up from our immortal souls, woven together by Altus.

Feel this angel, feel the ways that you live in it and with it and through it. Feel the way that you and your own angel are woven into the fibers of its being. This is another doorway to joy, to flood the loving places within with the energy of the angels, to awaken the joy that is our true nature. For they, the angels, are beings of love, and we humans are ultimately beings of joy. Together we weave the cosmos together. Together, we fulfill the purpose for which we were both created.

How To Feel the Presence of Father Earth

Beyond ancestors, beyond angels, we find the presence of our holy world. In the old days people encountered the Earth as a god, as a vast, embodied being of joy. When we do this again we men who love men will be able to walk the Earth fully alive, breathing fully alive, living all of our nights and days in a state of holy aliveness.

The following exercises can be done with your partner, and they can also be done alone or in groups, to weave our people together with Father Earth on every level. You can do them indoors, but they are best and most pleasureably done outside, in nature, in the midst of his beautiful body.

Place your hands on the earth. Close your eyes. Feel that your palms are open and you can breathe in the energy of the earth into your body through your hands. Fill your body with earth energy. Breathe your own energy back down through your hands into the earth. Get to know Father Earth this way and let him get to know you. Feel the life of the Earth in this way, and let him feel you. Feel his joy, let it fill you.

Sense the air around you. As you breathe in, feel that the air is entering your body to pleasure you, to make love to you. As you breathe out, feel that your breath is entering the air and making love to it. Know that the air is part of the body of the Earth. Whenever you breathe, you are his lover and he is yours.

As you walk, swing arms and legs and move your body through the air feeling that you are moving through the Earth's body over and over again, pleasuring him, becoming his lover at every moment.

Sit on the ground. Rock on your buttocks and press your asshole down onto the earth. Feel the energy of the earth rise up into your body. Feel the earth enter and spread out in you until it fills your entire body.

Roll onto your stomach. Send energy out of your cock, send it down into the earth. Make love to the earth this way. Pleasure him. Stretch out your arms and legs and embrace as much of his sacred body as you can. Let the Earth know how much you love and adore him.

Wallow in the dirt and mud of Father Earth's own body. Rub it all over yourself. Be covered by his dark, holy body. Paint yourself with his body. Take a stone and rub it all over yourself. Feel the Earth in the stone as you pleasure yourself, feel this god-cock touching every part of you and blessing you in a baptism by earth, by mud, by stone.

Walk in the rain. Walk naked in the rain. Feel that the god is coming all over you. Splash in streams. Swim. Feel the liquid body of the god all around you. Slip and slide through his body. Drink his body into your own. Let the waters of his body become one with you. Love yourself into him. Merge with him. Your body is mostly liquid. His body is ocean. Be ocean with him, surging and vast.

Every blade of grass, every bush, every tree, is another cock of Father Earth's body. When you eat, you are eating his body. Always feel this. Swallow his holy body and make it a part of your own. As you walk through the grass, the bushes, the trees, feel his erotic energy flowing up from the ground, brushing against you, caressing you, stroking you.

Find a tree that you love. Embrace it. Feel its power surging upwards. Wrap your arms around this tree and hold it close to you so that you can feel the magnificent life that flows through it. Remember, in the time of Tayarti, men who loved men were the guardians of the trees. To this day we meet in the trees as no other people do. Honor the trees. Pleasure the trees. Make love to the Earth through one of his many, many cocks. In this way you will get to know him better.

The Earth is alive. Feel his life. The earth is alive. Make love to him. In everything you do, feel the earth and make love to him. How many ways can you invent of your own to make love to the Earth? We are poised always between man and god. In this time, let us remember Father Earth. He has been called by many names. Call him what you will. But know that whatever you call him, alone, with partner, in our tribe, that your work is not separate from him. In truth, it all comes from him and goes back to him again. Our Earthly Father, divine child of our Heavenly Mother, through whose body we who are embodied come to know her, the Oneness from whom all that is arises. The beginning and end, the journey, the source, the giver of life, Creator of All.

Liturgies for Mother Sky

Some call the Creator of the universe God, but our earliest ancestors, when they looked in awe at the world around them and tried to understand where it came from, saw the ultimate creative force as Goddess, as Mother. The Father of our culture created the world by speaking it into existence. The Mother of our ancestors birthed the universe from her body. There was no separation between Creator and creation. And as we shift our thinking and come back to this ancient wisdom, we will find balance and healing for ourselves. Ultimately the Creator is neither male nor female, but Oneness. It is the Prime Vibration. It is Absolute Information. In seeing It as Mother we honor our own capacity for connection, compassion, clarity and communion of the soul. In knowing It as Mother we cycle back to the beginning of this era so that we can step into the next in wholeness.

The liturgies of the Father are spoken, as revelation comes from the Father in words, for with words he created the universe. The universe itself is the revelation of the Mother, and her liturgies are of the body. As we open to seeing her and her creation, as we learn to feel our place in it and know that we are never separate from it, and cannot ever be separate from it, then everything we do becomes a prayer. Anchored in love, our bodies filled with joy, reaching out in ecstasy to express our gratitude, we ground the Mother's bliss in the world.

In our Mother's world, we do not have to struggle for enlightenment. Her light is always with us. We do not have to be reborn, for each moment of our lives is a new creation in her infinite, eternal body, and we are always a part of it.

When you stretch in the morning as you roll up from sleeping, that is prayer. When you get out of bed and eat, that is celebration and sacrament. Each shower you take is a baptism, the work you do is always divine service, whatever it might be. When you dance, when you sing, you are offering your thanksgiving prayers to her. When you make love, Two Men Together, two flute players, when you enter into the darkness from which all things come, you are as close to her as ever you can get, birthing newness as she birthed the myriad children that are stars and worlds. And these are the liturgies of the Mother, chanted by joy-filled bodies, danced in holy celebration, in the midst of her divine aliveness.

A Day of Blessing

In the days of Tayarti, of Mayurdani and Namukra, of Akidrada, in the days of Kuniata and our ancient temples, our people celebrated the feast of the New Year at the time of the spring equinox. In the season of new birth, at the time when night and day are equal, the Walks-Between People would gather together to dance and sing, to tell our stories, to celebrate the entry of new men into our tribe, to rejoice in the love that two together came to share. We gathered in our villages and our encampments, in every part of the world. And in our own time, on the same day of the same season, when light and darkness are in balance, let the Walks-Between People gather again, to celebrate as a people.

Alone or with your partner, with your partner and with others, in a circle of trees or a circle within walls, come together to celebrate our Blessing Day.

Make yourselves an altar, a circular altar. In the center, on cloth or paper, draw for yourselves a circle and around it the signs of our clans. In the east, the home of the Scout clan, place a sprig of pine, a rose or a stick of incense, whose fragrance will call forth in you the scouting ways of our people. In the south, the home of the Flute Player clan, set down a clear glass bowl of water, a symbol of our clarity, our fluid creativity, our capacity for love. In the west, the home of the Shaman clan, place a single candle, whose flame will remind you of the strength of our people, of our endurance and of our courage to heal. In the north, the home of the Hunter clan, the place of spirit, put a single stone of any kind that calls to you, for we are hunters of spirit, and our journey as Walks-Between People is always a journey embodied on Earth, to be lived in harmony with all who dwell here.

Sit alone or with others of our people. We have our coming out days and rituals. This is a Coming In day, a coming in to who we are as a people. Inhale the fragrant branch or flower in the east, the place of new beginnings. May all that you breathe be fragrant, and may all your words and deeds be sweet and healing. May we work together to heal the air of this world. Sip the clear water of the south, the water of life. May you always be a fountain of love and life, may the gifts of our people be a gift to all who live here. And may the words and works of our lives as a people be a healing for the waters of this world. Light the fire of the west. Feel the heart-fire that burns within you. May our lives be an inspiration to each other and to the world. May our words and actions be a healing to the spark of divine life that manifests itself in all who dwell here. Take in your hands the stone of the north. Press it to your heart, warm it in your hands. This stone is the body of our Father Earth, on whose broad strong back we walk our mortal days. In all of our deeds and thoughts and dreams may we Walks-Between People be a healing to the Earth, a gift, a blessing.

All people are a blessing to the world. We are a blessing. All nations are a blessing to the world. We are a blessing. Like our sisters of the Woman Loving Nation, like the Blind and Deaf and other scouting peoples, we Men Who Love Men come together from all other peoples. On this day, let us sit together, stand together, walk together, sing together, feast together, dance together, in sweetness, creativity, inspiration and blessing, for ourselves and for all of the world to see and honor.

We Are Becoming Elders

When we live in balance, as body and spirit, as male and female, when we own our dark and our golden shadows, when we embrace and heal our inner child, then we are ready to begin the final stage in our Walks-Between journey, the journey to becoming elders.

In recent history there has been no one to tell us the stories of our people. We had no elders, no grandfathers, who could tell us who we are, why we are, or where we come from. Without our elders, we could not walk the earth in a grounded, healing way.

But now we are becoming elders. This journey we have been on is awakening in us our rich and ancient history. What began at the end of the last Ice Age is finding its fulfillment now, in our days. And together as a people again we are walking into the future, in truth, in pride, and in joy. We are becoming elders with and for each other, with and for the generations of gay men who will follow us. We are becoming elders with the elders who went before us, and with the angels who have guided our people since time began.

This is the work of joy, to become elders. This is the holy work we have struggled out of fear and hiding to do. We are remembering the stories of our people, and we are telling new ones. We are awakening the wisdom of our people, and we are adding to it. We are owning our powers as scouts, flute players, shamans and hunters, and we are sharing them with others in our tribe. We are remembering that we are midwives for the dying, guardians of the trees, that we are beauty makers and scouts in consciousness. As we come from all other peoples, born from their bodies and yet ourselves a people, we are peace makers, we are ambassadors from the future, who model for the rest of the world to see how human beings can live together in harmony and joy.

This is the holy work that we have been doing, the work of remembering, the work of becoming, the work of celebrating who we are as sons of Father Earth and Mother Sky. We are blessed by our parents, and we are a blessing to the world. We are the Walks-Between People, between matter and spirit, female and male, night and day, wisdom and innocence, joy and sorrow. What we walk between we contain. What we contain is who we are, and who we are is all and everything.

Let us sit now in our elderhood. Alone and with our partners, with our partners and in community. Let us sit now and tell our stories, sing our songs and dance our dances. We are becoming elders. Old and wise, strong and beautiful, we awaken joy in our bodies and we share it with the world. For this we were created by Mother Sky and Father Earth. This is our heritage, this is our destiny. We are a blessing to ourselves, a blessing to our lovers, a blessing to our people, and a blessing to the world.

The Song of Two Flutes Together

The journey is all there is. The journey to love, the journey to joy, the journey to wisdom. The journey Home. I touch you. You touch me. We touch each other. We dance. I whisper these words to you. You whisper words back to me. We hunger. We seek. And yet, what is it that we seek?

Enlightenment is wordless, my beloved. Too vast to be spoken. How can it be expressed? Only the tongue gliding over your skin can say it. Wordless, pressing syllables over your lips, pressing silence into you.

This is the only way to speak these things. These teachings, how can they be only about the mind? Where does the mind stop and the body begin? I run my hands down your side. Where do you feel me? In the neural wires of your brain, or in strong bearing of your hips?

No, only the wordless slip of my tongue down the left side of your neck, onto shoulder, chest, talking parables around your taut right nipple, then chanting my way down to your navel. No, only my tongue playing over each night-dark hair like the strings of a cello, bound to your body at one end, and stretching out to heaven on the other, only this silent concerto can begin to express the infinite words of the great transmission. Yes. Like fire, words crackle between our skin. Your mouth glides down to meet me. Songs, poems, hymns, pass back and forth from tongue to river-wet tongue. There are no choruses in this chant. No repetition. Each verse is whole unto itself. Each verse is all of God's creation. All seven days compressed into one fiery instant, that rebirths itself endlessly into our flesh.

The breath. The rise and fall of your breath. Ribs compressing and then expanding. Paragraph after paragraph. My fingers reading all of them. Holding all of them. Dropping mouth once again to eat them. Word upon word. Holy wisdom of body screaming its pleasures into us.

Rolling over, the universe itself rolls over. Sutra after sutra tumbling and rewriting itself. The weight of your body on top of me surges up oceans of verse, encyclopedic. Calling to God, my body the psalm that you stretch out upon. Altar. Scripture. Book after book laid open to your eyes.

Your eyes, vast as night. I fall into them. As you fall into mine. Everything rises in this falling. Body, breath, bard-music. Written across the sheets of your bed, page after page of it. Beloved, this is the great transmission of wisdom. This is the mystery the ancients knew and shared. This is the wordless secret of the ages. Your tongue on fire in my mouth. Burning your liquid sentences into my infinite body-brain's perfect spiral notebook.

For you are the divine beloved. You are the immortal son of Father Earth. You are the source of illumination in the world. You are the holy one of days gone by. You are the divine beloved. You are the source of enlightenment in the world. You are man, woman, child, dolphin, angel. You are the holy parent of days to come. Son of Mother Sky. Beloved priest in her galactic temple.

So I reach out my hand to you, beloved one. As you reach out hand to me. And where we touch, music happens. Let us begin there. Let us begin with the sound. Two flutes play. Water pours over itself, in the confluence of two streams. Candle burns beside candle. Their flames merge, lighting a darkened room. Two flutes play. Their notes circle in and around each other. This is the way of man-loving-man love. A special love. Deep, ancient, and ours to explore, my holy friend. Ours to explore, my brothers of the Walks-Between People, in the temple of day after day and night after night.

Tayarti's Peace-Light Prayer

Mother of all,
*   open our hearts.*
Mother of all,
*   fill us with wisdom.*
May our love be a fountain
*   that cleanses the world.*
May all be washed clean,
*   be washed pure,*
*   be made whole again.*
Through our love,
*   which is Your nature,*
Through our love,
*   which is Your name.*
Mother of all,
*   a thousand blessings.*

Peace peace peace peace peace peace forever.

Acknowledgments

A book has many parents, especially one that took fifteen years to write. In addition to its non-physical fathers, Yamati, Arrasu and Sargolais, I want to honor the following, no longer in physical bodies: my father Jack who first led me to think that gay men have a history worth remembering, and Lois Hart, Dedalus Brooks-Smith, Dennis Florio, Cameron Duncan, Fred Stahl, Tony Losi, Joseph McKay, John Fletcher Harris, Gerard Rizza, Randy Wickstrom, Terry Weisser, Raven Wolfdancer, Jeff Wadlington, David Vincent, Neville Rowe, Mark Honaker and Mark Walker. I also want to express my gratitude to the following for their inspiration: Barbara Shor, Charles Lawrence, Joan Larkin, Stuart Schear, Carol Robin, Bonnie Gintis, Don Shewey. And to Joel Czarlinsky, Davidson Lloyd, Tom Keegan and the men in the 1986 gay healing and meditation group. And to Samuel Kirschner, Nelson Bloncourt, Annie Sprinkle and everyone from the New York Healing Circle. To the men who took my workshops in Key West and Oakland. To Michel Schummer, Johannes Muller, Martin Raffael Siems and the men who took my workshops in Klein Sachau and Heidelberg. To John Stowe, Monty Schuth, Peter Kendricks, Rocco Patt, Franklin Abbott, Ron Lambe, King Thackston, Jonathan Lerner, Duncan Teague, Al Cotton, David-Michael Searcy, Jay Beard, Gary Kaupman, Raphael Sabbatini, Bernhard Zinkgraf, Todd Kinney, Martin Isganitis, Dandelion and all the other wonderful men from the Gay Spirit Visions Conference. And to Harry Hay, Stephen Palmer, Gary Plouff, John Pasqualetti, Danny Pietryk, Kerry Blasdel, Mark Thompson, Thomas Barnes, Matthew Simmons. And to Michael Starkman, and Larry Hermsen, and most especially to Joseph Kramer, for publishing the first sections of this book in its several incarnations, and to Colin Brown and Body Electric also, for keeping it out in the world. And lastly, my deep, deep gratitude to Bert Herrman of Alamo Square Press, for believing in this curious little volume.

The new edition of this book exists because of the support and encouragement of Toby Johnson, Bo Young, and Dan Vera of *White Crane*, and the support and commitment of Steve Berman at Lethe Press. I want to thank San Francisco artist Paul Jerrman for the beautiful image on the cover of this book. You can see more of his work at pauljerrman.com, and Michael Starkman, who led me to Paul's work and was instrumental in getting the book out in the world in the first place, all those years ago.

The Heartland Men's Chorus of Kansas City, Missouri commissioned composer and lyricist Mark Hayes to create a fifty-minute song cycle for them to perform. It premiered in 2002. Mark used text from the book and wrote additional lyrics inspired by it. Copies can be ordered of the CD, "Two Flutes Playing," at the chorus's website: www.hmckc.org.

Thank you all.

LaVergne, TN USA
15 March 2010
176022LV00001B/66/A